contents

Having dedicated years to instilling a love of cooking among our readers, it is gratifying to now have produced a beginners' cookbook. Among other things, cooking teaches you that timing is everything; it develops your organisational skills and nurtures your self-confidence – all in all, it's simply applied commonsense. Nothing scary in that. Take this book to your heart as well as your tastebuds... it was compiled with our great enthusiasm for keeping cooking alive and well and living in kitchens all over the country.

Pamela Clark

Food Director

before you start...

Cooking is neither difficult nor unfathomable. With a little experience – and this book – you will find yourself increasingly developing new skills and gaining greater confidence in the kitchen. Here, we've compiled some general information to help answer some of the "whys", "hows" and "whats" that may arise about the methods and instructions you read in these pages. Plus, you'll find some relevant illustrated techniques and, at the back, our handy glossary. With *Beginners Cooking Class*, you'll quickly discover that cooking for yourself, family and friends is not just more economical and nutritional than buying takeaway or pre-prepared foods, but also creative, intriguing, satisfying... and a lot of fun.

The first thing to do before starting to cook is to read the recipe through from beginning to end: you may not have every one of the essential ingredients; you need to know beforehand if overnight marinating is necessary; and there could be a recipe within a recipe that has to be made ahead of time. Be prepared – a clear understanding of the recipe's requirements before you begin sets you free to travel down the road to culinary success.

use authentic ingredients

Visit specialist grocers and greengrocers if necessary to purchase authentic ingredients. It follows that the reason you've come to love various ethnic dishes in the first place is probably because you tasted them in a restaurant specialising in a particular country's cuisine (or perhaps you were even lucky enough to taste the food in its country of origin) where, naturally, the ingredients were authentic. Wherever possible, always use the freshest, best-quality ingredients you can find. It's false economy to cut corners on the content: always remember that, with cooking, the whole is greater than the sum of its parts – what chance have you got if the "parts" don't measure up in the first place?

learning to wok

Carbon-steel and cast-iron woks must be "seasoned" (readied for cooking) before they're used for the first time. First, wash your wok in hot, soapy water to remove all traces of grease, then dry it thoroughly. Place the wok on the stove over high heat; when hot, rub about 1 tablespoon of cooking oil over all of the inside surface with absorbent paper. Continue heating the wok for 10 minutes, wiping from time to time with a ball of clean absorbent paper. This treatment creates a certain amount of smoke because you're effectively "burning off" the oil; make certain you're holding both the wok and the paper you're wiping it with wearing oven gloves. Repeat this whole process twice – your wok is now ready to use. When using a wok, there's no reason to rinse or wipe it out between additions of ingredients, since they all contribute to the flavour of the finished dish. It is a good idea, however, to wipe out the wok, using dry absorbent paper, once you've completed cooking one recipe before you begin to stir-fry another for the same meal. When you've finished cooking, clean the wok with hot water and a nylon scrubber or other non-abrasive scourer: avoid using soap if possible so that you don't "wash away" the seasoned surface, which improves with use. Dry the wok thoroughly before putting it away: placing it over low heat for a minute or two is the best method – however, don't forget and walk away while it's over the heat!

cooking with wine

Never cook with a wine that tastes "off" or one that has been open for more than a few days. A good rule of thumb when selecting a wine that's to be used in a marinade or as an ingredient, is that if a wine's not good enough to drink, it's not good enough to cook with! Many cooks serve the same wine that they've used in the dish for continuity of flavour. If you prefer not to use wine at all, substitute stock, water, fruit juice or liqueur – whatever is appropriate.

why marinate?

Marinades not only impart their flavour to an ingredient but, in the case of meat, they also help in tenderising it. While we give a general time-frame of "3 hours to overnight" for marinating, ideally you should always marinate as close to the maximum 24-hour period as possible, to achieve a true depth of flavour.

taste for seasoning

When using commercially prepared stocks, pastes, salsas or pestos, use care before adding other seasoning – packaged products can be very salty. Perform your own taste-test first before reaching for the salt.

it's all in the timing

The preparation and cooking times we give at the top of each recipe are guidelines only. We've factored in extra time knowing that this is, after all, a cookbook for beginners, so don't be surprised or concerned if, after a few attempts, you find you're finishing the recipe in less time than we suggest... with experience, we expect that you will. We also expect that you will have read the recipe through and gathered together all the required ingredients before you actually begin: that's when our preparation time begins, too.

knowing your equipment

The type of cookware you use and the idiosyncrasies of your stove all impact on the finished product. Cooking times will vary (albeit marginally) depending on whether you use an electric or gas oven, and on the material of which your saucepans and baking dishes are made. With a watchful eye and a little time, you'll quickly learn how your equipment performs.

get to know your ingredients

SPAGHETTI

Different pasta shapes suit different sauces: as a rule, the longer the pasta, the thinner the sauce; short and fat, or hollow, pasta best suits thick meat or vegetable sauces.

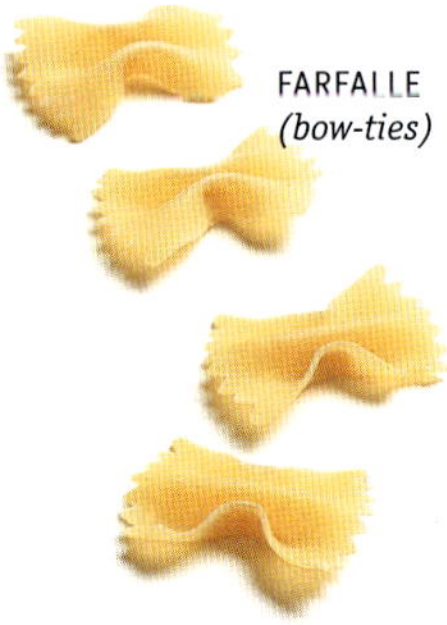

FARFALLE
(bow-ties)

ORECCHIETTE
(little ears)

FUSILLI
(spirals or screws)

PENNE
(quills)

Most potato types are best suited to a particular cooking method: pink-eye and new are good for salads; kipfler makes great wedges; and orange-fleshed kumara is beautiful pureed.

No other ingredient imparts such authentic flavour to a dish as the appropriate fresh herb: if cooking a traditional Italian casserole, say so with the taste of basil or oregano; when making a Thai curry, don't forget the coriander and lemon grass; add chives, the parsleys and mint when crossing culinary borders between Europe, North Africa, the Middle East and beyond.

Identifying one herb from another or choosing the right spud for a particular use doesn't take a culinary Einstein... just a keen cook with a good eye, a dollop of curiosity and a hefty dose of basic commonsense.

ROCKET

BABY SPINACH

SILVERBEET *(Swiss chard)*

CURLY ENDIVE

We are spoilt for choice these days, given the vast number of different-tasting (yet always delicious) green-leafed salad vegetables that can be found in almost every greengrocer and supermarket.

Chillies add flavour as well as heat so don't be afraid to give them a go. To lessen their intensity, seed before using.

RED THAI CHILLIES

Asian greens are now commonplace on our daily menus, adding not only unique flavour to stir-fry combinations but also providing a delicious new take on the old concept of meat and three veg.

a few helpful techniques...

measuring dry ingredients

Use a graduated set (a 1/4-, 1/3-, 1/2- and 1-cup nest) of cups when measuring dry ingredients: fill required-size cup then level off the top with a palette knife.

separating an egg

Always break eggs one at a time into a bowl: if one is stale, you won't ruin the others. Tap cold eggs gently against side of a bowl then use both hands to separate.

successfully beating egg whites

Use dry, grease-free utensils to beat room temperature egg whites, watching for the forming of "soft" peaks, those that literally "fall over" when beaters are lifted.

roasting and peeling capsicums

Quarter capsicum; discard seeds and membrane. Roast or grill, skin-side up, until skin blisters and blackens; cover pieces in plastic for 5 minutes, peel away skin.

preparing fresh asparagus

Bend lower third of asparagus spear: the end will snap off between the woody base and the flesh of the spear. You may like to peel the thicker, tougher spears.

peeling tomatoes

Core then cut a shallow cross in tomato base; cover with boiling water in heatproof bowl, stand about 2 minutes. Peel away skin, from cross end toward top.

peeling garlic

Separate garlic cloves then, using the side of a large heavy knife, press down firmly, slightly crushing the individual cloves: the skin will fall away from the garlic.

chopping onions finely

Halve peeled onion lengthways; keep root end intact. Using sharp knife, grip onion and slice thinly, first down the length then across, in crosshatch pattern.

eggs

for your information...

To assist in shelling hard-boiled eggs, remove them from boiling water, crack the shells all over and immediately plunge eggs into a bowl of cold water. This helps prevent the yolk from discolouring, halts any further cooking and speeds up the cooling process, making the eggs easier to shell.

Exercise caution when it comes to using raw egg in recipes (like in dressings or mayonnaise) – your local authorities can advise you if there is a salmonella problem in your area.

The best egg is as fresh an egg as possible: if in doubt about its freshness, try the following test. Place the uncooked egg carefully in a bowl containing enough cold water to cover the egg: if it sinks, it's fresh, if it floats, don't use it. Never use an egg that has been cracked for some time before it is to be used.

Before using them in a recipe, break eggs, one at a time, into a small cup or onto a saucer. That way, if an egg is stale, it can be simply discarded, rather than ruin the whole dish.

Crowding eggs in pan so they don't crack

boiled eggs

COOKING TIME 5-15 MINUTES

4 eggs

1 Use a saucepan in which the eggs will fit fairly snugly, to avoid them cracking while they are boiling. Place eggs in pan; add enough cold water to just cover eggs.

2 Place pan, covered, over high heat; when water boils, uncover pan but allow water to continue to boil. Timing the eggs is a fairly personal matter but, for a 60g egg, 3 minutes will result in a soft-boiled egg having a runny yolk and barely set white, 5 minutes will produce an egg with a firm white and yolk beginning to set solid, and 10 minutes will result in a hard-boiled egg.

per egg 5.3g fat; 309kJ

scrambled eggs

PREPARATION TIME 3 MINUTES • COOKING TIME 3 MINUTES

Add any chopped herb you like to the eggs instead of our suggested chives.

4 eggs
1/3 cup milk (80ml)
1 tablespoon finely chopped fresh chives
1 teaspoon butter

1 Break eggs, 1 at a time, into a cup or onto a saucer. Place eggs together in small bowl; using a whisk, beat lightly. Add milk and chives; whisk to combine.

2 Melt butter in medium saucepan over low heat; add egg mixture. When egg mixture starts to "catch" on bottom of pan, begin gently stirring it, continuously, with a wooden spoon. Cook only until egg is just firm.

SERVES 2

per serve 15g fat; 837kJ

serving suggestions Scrambled eggs are delicious with bacon or sausages and toast, but they are also great served on toasted brioche with smoked salmon and cucumber – or on toasted sourdough bread with garlic butter.

Adding milk to eggs

Stirring egg mixture with a wooden spoon

tips

- Whisk the eggs just long enough to combine the yolks and whites; excessive beating will aerate the mixture too much.
- Scrambled eggs should be eaten as soon as they have finished cooking because they become unpalatable very quickly.

zucchini and mushroom omelette

PREPARATION TIME 10 MINUTES • COOKING TIME 10 MINUTES

Adding zucchini to mushrooms and garlic

Whisking cheese into the egg mixture

Pouring the egg mixture into pan

Flipping half of the omelette to cover filling

2 teaspoons butter
1 clove garlic, crushed
25g button mushrooms, sliced thinly
¼ cup coarsely grated zucchini (50g)
1 green onion, chopped finely
2 eggs
1 tablespoon water
¼ cup coarsely grated cheddar cheese (30g)

1 Heat 1 teaspoon of the butter in a small non-stick frying pan; cook garlic and mushrooms, stirring, over medium heat about 2 minutes or until mushrooms are just browned. Add zucchini and onion; cook, stirring, about 1 minute or until zucchini begins to soften. Remove vegetable mixture from pan; cover to keep warm.

2 Break eggs, 1 at a time, into a cup or onto a saucer. Place eggs together in small bowl with the water; using a whisk, beat lightly. Add cheese; whisk until combined.

3 Heat remaining butter in same pan; swirl pan so butter covers base. Pour egg mixture into pan; cook, tilting pan, over medium heat until almost set.

4 Place vegetable mixture evenly over half of the omelette; using eggslice, flip other half over vegetable mixture. Using eggslice, slide omelette gently onto serving plate.

SERVES 1

per serve 29.2g fat; 1502kJ

tips

- Assemble and prepare all of the ingredients before beginning to cook.
- You can use a regular frying pan, but spray the pan with cooking-oil spray before adding the egg mixture.
- The frying pan and butter should be quite hot when the egg mixture is added, so the omelette base sets almost immediately.
- If you prefer a plain omelette, omit the vegetables and cheese.
- You can use any type of cheese in place of the cheddar, or substitute the mushrooms and zucchini with baby spinach leaves and chopped fried bacon, or finely chopped raw tomato and onion. Two tablespoons of your favourite chopped herbs will enliven almost every omelette.

tips

- We prefer to oven-cook frittata because it doesn't require the same attention as one cooked on top of the stove.
- If cooking frittata on a stove-top, once the eggs are almost set, place the frying pan briefly under a hot grill to lightly brown the top. You can also brown an oven-cooked frittata this way, but only if you're using a flameproof dish or pan.
- You can fill a frittata with almost anything: try ham and tomatoes; spinach; or anchovies, garlic and tomatoes.

rocket, potato and bacon frittata

PREPARATION TIME 10 MINUTES • COOKING TIME 50 MINUTES (plus cooling time)

A frittata is the Italian version of a flat omelette. Cooked slowly in the oven or on top of the stove over low heat, a frittata is often cut into squares and used as a sandwich filling, and is just as likely to be eaten cold as hot.

2 medium potatoes (400g)
2 bacon rashers, chopped coarsely
1 medium brown onion (150g), chopped finely
1 clove garlic, crushed
50g baby rocket leaves, chopped coarsely
6 eggs, whisked lightly
3/4 cup sour cream (180ml)

1 Preheat oven to moderate. Grease deep 20cm round cake pan.

2 Boil, steam or microwave peeled whole potatoes until tender; cool, slice thinly.

3 Meanwhile cook bacon in small frying pan until browned. Add onion and garlic; cook, stirring, until onion is soft. Remove pan from heat; stir in rocket.

4 Place half of the bacon mixture over base of prepared cake pan, top with half the potato, remaining bacon mixture then remaining potato. Pour combined egg and sour cream carefully over bacon and potato; bake in moderate oven about 35 minutes or until frittata is set and just cooked through.

5 Brown top of frittata under hot grill, if desired. Stand cooked frittata 2 minutes before serving.

SERVES 4

per serve 29.2g fat; 1649kJ

Slicing the cooked potatoes thinly

Adding onion and garlic to the bacon

Lightly whisking eggs

caesar salad

PREPARATION TIME 15 MINUTES • COOKING TIME 5 MINUTES

This salad is thought to have originated in the 1920s in Tijuana, Mexico, in a restaurant owned by Italian chef Caesar Cardini. The dressing recipe contains an uncooked egg; if local health authorities caution against eating raw eggs, simply omit it, or poach an extra egg and process it with the other dressing ingredients.

Browning the croutons in batches

7 slices thick white bread
2 tablespoons light olive oil
100g parmesan cheese
1 large cos lettuce
5 canned whole anchovy fillets, drained, halved lengthways
4 eggs

CAESAR DRESSING

1 egg
1 clove garlic, crushed
2 tablespoons lemon juice
1/2 teaspoon Dijon mustard
5 canned whole anchovy fillets, drained
3/4 cup light olive oil (180ml)

1 Discard crusts from bread; cut bread into 2cm cubes. Heat oil in large frying pan; cook bread, in batches, stirring, until browned and crisp. Drain croutons on absorbent paper.

2 Using vegetable peeler, shave cheese into long thin pieces.

3 Combine torn lettuce leaves with half of the croutons, half of the anchovies and half of the cheese in large bowl; add half of the dressing, mix well. Sprinkle remaining croutons, anchovies and cheese over salad; drizzle with remaining dressing. Divide salad among serving plates.

4 Half fill a shallow frying pan with water; bring to a boil. Break eggs, 1 at a time, into a small bowl, then slide each egg into the pan. When all eggs are in the pan, allow water to return to a boil. Cover pan, turn off heat; stand about 4 minutes or until a light film of egg white has set over yolks.

5 Remove eggs, 1 at a time, using an eggslice; place egg, still on eggslice, on absorbent-paper-lined saucer to blot up any poaching liquid. Place 1 egg on each serving plate.

caesar dressing Blend or process egg, garlic, juice, mustard and anchovies until smooth; with motor operating, add oil in thin stream, process until dressing thickens.

SERVES 4

per serve 75.6g fat; 3953kJ

Shaving the parmesan into long thin pieces

Sliding egg into pan

Placing egg on absorbent paper

tips

- When poaching the eggs, cover the pan with a glass lid so you can keep an eye on the poaching process. Don't lift the lid during poaching – steam helps set the eggs.
- For those who don't like pieces of anchovy lurking among the lettuce leaves, try processing all the anchovies in the dressing mixture.
- Many restaurants add grilled chicken breast pieces to Caesar salad, to make the meal more substantial.

tips

- Caster sugar is quick and easy to dissolve; test that the sugar is totally dissolved by rubbing a small amount of the meringue between your fingers; if you can feel the sugar grains, the mixture needs additional beating, on high speed, until it feels silky smooth.
- The egg whites should be at room temperature before starting to add the sugar.
- Use spotlessly clean beaters for this recipe; any trace of grease prevents the egg whites from rising to the required volume. For the same reason, when separating the eggs, make sure no yolk is included with the whites.
- The fruit used to top a pavlova is dependent on seasonal availability, although the classic pavlova recipe usually contains mixed berries and passionfruit pulp. Our version uses carambola, nectarine, green apple, strawberries and raspberries.

pavlova

PREPARATION TIME 15 MINUTES
COOKING TIME 1 HOUR 30 MINUTES

Both Australia and New Zealand claim to be the country of origin of this famous meringue, cream and fruit dessert, but both countries agree it was named after the Russian prima ballerina, Anna Pavlova.

4 egg whites
1 cup caster sugar
300ml thickened cream
3 cups chopped fresh mixed fruit

1 Preheat oven to very slow. Cover a greased oven tray with a piece of baking paper.

2 Place egg whites in small clean dry bowl; using an electric mixer, beat on high speed about 1 minute or until soft peaks form. Gradually add sugar, about 1 tablespoon at a time, beating well after each addition, until sugar dissolves; scrape any sugar crystals from side of bowl with rubber spatula.

3 Spoon meringue into a round shape approximately 20cm in diameter on the prepared oven tray; level top of meringue gently and slightly with a rubber spatula. Bake, uncovered, in very slow oven about $1\frac{1}{2}$ hours or until meringue feels firm and dry to the touch. Turn oven off; open oven door and leave ajar to cool meringue slowly in oven.

4 Place cream in small bowl; using an electric mixer, beat on medium speed until soft peaks form.

5 Turn meringue onto serving platter so base faces upwards; top with cream and fruit.

SERVES 6

per serve meringue only 0g fat; 629kJ

pavlova 19g fat; 1482kJ

Adding sugar gradually to egg whites

Spooning meringue onto the oven tray

Levelling the meringue with a spatula

Placing meringue on serving plate

pasta, rice and

for your information...

Different pasta shapes suit different sauces: generally, the longer the pasta, the thinner the sauce. Spaghetti suits butter-based white sauces or creamy tomato sauces; spiral pasta suits thick cream or meat sauces; spaghettini (thin spaghetti) is best with seafood sauces or sauces with a lot of olive oil, as it clings to the long strands; short, fat pasta should be served with thick meat or vegetable sauces; and ribbon pastas, like fettuccine, go best with rich butter, cream or cheese sauces.

Pasta cooking times vary, plus cooks have their own ideas about the right degree of tenderness. For dried pasta, follow the packet directions, but test 1 to 2 minutes short of the suggested cooking time. Fresh pasta – and noodles – are a different matter, with some needing no pre-cooking whatsoever and others requiring that you rinse them in hot water or soak them for a brief period. Follow the recipe method or manufacturer's instructions for individual types.

To reheat pasta, pour boiling water over it while in a colander, placed over a large saucepan. Separate pasta pieces with a fork, then lift colander from pan to drain.

pasta with boscaiola sauce

PREPARATION TIME 10 MINUTES • COOKING TIME 20 MINUTES

Boscaiola means "in the style of a forest-dweller", presumably because a stroll through the woods often yields great numbers of edible mushrooms, an essential ingredient in this sauce.

2 teaspoons olive oil
200g button mushrooms, sliced thickly
2 cloves garlic, crushed
200g ham, chopped coarsely
1/4 cup dry white wine (60ml)
300ml cream
500g pasta
2 tablespoons finely chopped fresh chives

Adding mushrooms to pan

Adding wine to mushroom mixture

1 Heat oil in a medium saucepan; cook mushrooms, garlic and ham, stirring, until ingredients are lightly browned. Add wine; boil, uncovered, until wine reduces by half.

2 Add cream to mushroom mixture; simmer, uncovered, until sauce thickens slightly.

3 Meanwhile, cook pasta in large saucepan of boiling water, uncovered, until just tender; drain.

4 Add chives and pasta to sauce, using salad servers or a pasta fork. Toss gently until mixed and heated through.

SERVES 4

per serve 32.6g fat; 3294kJ

noodles

tips

- Experiment with any mushroom variety. We used button mushrooms.
- Substitute chicken stock or milk for the wine if you wish – or leave it out for a thicker sauce.
- Use lean leg ham to reduce fat.
- Serve with any pasta – fresh is best. Experiment with flavoured fettuccines, available fresh and dried.

vegetarian lasagne

PREPARATION TIME 40 MINUTES • COOKING TIME 1 HOUR 50 MINUTES

2 medium eggplants (600g)
coarse cooking salt
2 tablespoons olive oil
2 medium red capsicums (400g)
$1\frac{1}{2}$ cups bottled tomato pasta sauce (375g)
250g instant lasagne sheets
$\frac{3}{4}$ cup coarsely grated mozzarella cheese (75g)
$\frac{1}{2}$ cup pesto (135g)
$\frac{1}{2}$ cup finely grated parmesan cheese (40g)

WHITE SAUCE
60g butter
$\frac{1}{4}$ cup plain flour (35g)
$1\frac{1}{2}$ cups milk (375ml)
$\frac{1}{2}$ cup finely grated parmesan cheese (40g)

1 Oil a 2-litre (8-cup) rectangular baking dish.

2 Cut unpeeled eggplants into 1cm slices. Place in colander, sprinkle all over with salt; stand 30 minutes. Preheat oven to moderately hot.

3 Rinse eggplant well under cold water; pat dry with absorbent paper. Brush eggplant with oil; place, in single layer, on two oven trays. Cook, uncovered, in moderately hot oven about 40 minutes or until browned and tender.

4 Meanwhile, quarter capsicums, remove seeds and membranes. Roast under grill or in a very hot oven, skin-side up, until skin blisters and blackens. Cover capsicum pieces with plastic or paper for 5 minutes; peel away skin, cut capsicum into thick strips.

5 Lower oven temperature to moderate.

6 Spread one-third of the pasta sauce into prepared baking dish. Top with one-third of the lasagne sheets, another third of the sauce, half of the eggplant, half of the mozzarella; repeat layering, using another third of the lasagne sheets, remaining sauce, all of the capsicum, and remaining mozzarella, lasagne and eggplant. Spread pesto over eggplant; top with white sauce. Bake, covered, in moderate oven 30 minutes; uncover, sprinkle lasagne with parmesan, bake about 30 minutes longer or until browned. Remove from oven; stand, uncovered, about 5 minutes before serving.

white sauce Melt butter in medium saucepan; add flour, stir over heat until bubbling and grainy. Remove pan from heat, gradually stir in milk; stir over heat until mixture boils and thickens. Remove pan from heat; stir in cheese.

SERVES 6

per serve 31.6g fat; 2342kJ

Covering pasta sauce with lasagne sheets

Arranging eggplant over sauce

Making white sauce

Topping lasagne with white sauce

tips

- This lasagne will be even better if you make your own pesto and your own tomato sauce: see the recipes on pages 38 and 24 respectively.
- You can substitute zucchini, spinach or leek for the eggplant – each vegetable should be individually cooked before being layered.
- If you can, use fresh lasagne in preference to the dried version, or even use the fresh rice noodle sheets available from Asian supermarkets.

tomato sauce

Here are three variations for homemade tomato pasta sauce. For four people, we recommend serving 500g of pasta with your choice of sauce, accompanied by a green salad and a warm loaf of ciabatta or a French stick. Prepare the pasta by cooking it in a large saucepan of boiling water, uncovered, until just tender or "al dente", as the Italians say.

Adding basil to the canned-tomato sauce

Roasting tomato halves

Chopping olives for the uncooked sauce

...using canned tomatoes

PREPARATION TIME 10 MINUTES
COOKING TIME 20 MINUTES

1 tablespoon olive oil
1 medium brown onion (150g), chopped finely
2 cloves garlic, crushed
2 x 400g cans whole tomatoes
1/2 cup water (125ml)
1/2 cup vegetable stock (125ml)
1 tablespoon tomato paste
1 teaspoon sugar
2 tablespoons finely chopped fresh basil leaves

1 Heat oil in large frying pan; cook onion and garlic, stirring, until onion is softened.

2 Stir in undrained crushed tomatoes, water, stock, paste and sugar; bring to boil. Simmer, uncovered, about 15 minutes or until sauce thickens slightly. Stir in basil just before serving with hot pasta.

SERVES 4

per serve 5.6g fat; 537kJ (excluding pasta)

...using roasted fresh tomatoes

PREPARATION TIME 10 MINUTES
COOKING TIME 1 HOUR 15 MINUTES

1 tablespoon balsamic vinegar
2 teaspoons brown sugar
1 clove garlic, crushed
1 tablespoon olive oil
6 large egg tomatoes (540g), halved
20g butter
1 medium red onion (170g), chopped finely
1/2 cup water (125ml)
1/4 cup dry red wine (60ml)
1 tablespoon tomato paste
1/4 cup coarsely chopped fresh flat-leaf parsley
8 torn fresh basil leaves

1 Combine vinegar, sugar, garlic and oil in small jug; stir until sugar dissolves.

2 Place tomato halves, cut-side up, in medium flameproof baking dish; drizzle with vinegar mixture. Cook, uncovered, in hot oven about 50 minutes or until tomato is browned and softened.

3 Remove tomato from dish. Melt butter in same dish over low heat, add onion; cook, stirring, until onion is softened.

4 Return tomato to dish; stir in combined water, wine and paste. Bring to boil; simmer, uncovered, about 10 minutes or until thickened slightly, stirring occasionally. Stir in parsley and basil just before serving with hot pasta.

SERVES 4

per serve 9.4g fat; 539kJ (excluding pasta)

...using uncooked fresh tomatoes

PREPARATION TIME 20 MINUTES

6 medium egg tomatoes (450g)
1 medium white onion (150g), chopped finely
1/4 cup pimiento-stuffed green olives (35g), chopped finely
1 tablespoon drained capers, chopped finely
1/3 cup finely chopped fresh parsley
2 cloves garlic, crushed
1/2 cup olive oil (125ml)

1 Chop tomatoes into very fine dice; combine tomato in medium bowl with remaining ingredients.

2 Cover sauce; refrigerate overnight.

3 Serve, without heating, over hot pasta.

SERVES 4

per serve 30.6g fat; 1247kJ (excluding pasta)

tips

- This sauce should be made the day before you intend to serve it, to allow the flavours to meld.
- If you're not fond of pimiento-stuffed olives or capers, you can leave either – or both – out and substitute with 1/4 cup of finely shredded fresh basil leaves.
- Use any kind of tomatoes, but make sure that they're still firm – if they're overripe, they'll crush into a pulpy mass when you try to chop them.
- The olive oil is an important ingredient in this recipe, so use a good-quality extra virgin olive oil.

lemon risotto

PREPARATION TIME 15 MINUTES • COOKING TIME 40 MINUTES

This simple recipe proves preparing a risotto is not difficult, just time-consuming. Once you discover how easy a risotto is to make, and how versatile and delicious the basic recipe is, you'll be devising a different version every day of the week!

Adding rind and juice to stock and wine

1 litre chicken stock (4 cups)
1 cup dry white wine (250ml)
2 teaspoons finely grated lemon rind
1 tablespoon lemon juice
80g butter
1 medium brown onion (150g), chopped finely
2 cups arborio rice (400g)
3/4 cup finely grated parmesan cheese (60g)
2 tablespoons finely chopped fresh flat-leaf parsley

1. Bring stock and wine to boil in medium saucepan, add rind and juice; simmer, covered, while preparing onion and rice.
2. Heat half of the butter in large saucepan; cook onion, stirring, until soft. Add rice; stir over medium heat until coated in butter mixture and slightly changed in colour.
3. Uncover stock mixture; add 1 cup to rice mixture. Cook, stirring, over medium heat until liquid is absorbed.
4. Continue adding stock mixture, 1 cup at a time, stirring constantly, until liquid is absorbed between additions. Total cooking time should be about 35 minutes or until rice is just tender.
5. Remove pan from heat; stir in remaining butter, cheese and parsley. Serve immediately.

SERVES 4

per serve 22.1g fat; 2805kJ

tips

- Available in most supermarkets, arborio rice is a short fat white rice capable of absorbing several times its weight in liquid.
- You can use olive oil rather than butter, or equal amounts of each.
- The stock mixture is kept simmering as the risotto cooks because frequent additions of cold liquid lengthen the cooking time and startle the rice into being chewy.
- Buy the best quality parmesan you can and grate it yourself.
- Never make a risotto ahead – it will be gluey, heavy and unpalatable.

Coating rice in butter mixture

Adding hot stock to rice

The following variations can be made in practically the same time as the lemon risotto; simply omit the lemon rind and juice from the main recipe and add the suggested ingredients as directed.

risotto milanese

This risotto is usually served with osso buco (see recipe page 62).

Cook 50g finely chopped prosciutto and 1/2 teaspoon chopped saffron threads with the onion in step 2; omit the parsley in this version.

per serve 23.8g fat; 2911kJ

mushroom risotto

Cook 200g thickly sliced Swiss brown mushrooms and 200g thickly sliced cup mushrooms in 20g butter in medium saucepan, covered, over low heat until just soft; gently stir into risotto with the cheese and parsley.

per serve 27g fat; 3055kJ

pea and pancetta risotto

Cook 80g finely chopped pancetta with the onion in step 2; gently stir 1/2 cup (60g) thawed frozen peas into almost finished risotto with the last cup of stock mixture.

per serve 25g fat; 3001kJ

asparagus risotto

Boil, steam or microwave 500g trimmed and coarsely chopped fresh asparagus until just tender. Gently stir into risotto with the cheese; omit the parsley.

per serve 22.3g fat; 2893kJ

Cutting tofu into squares

Deveining prawns

Adding noodles to boiling water

Cooking tofu until golden brown

Adding prawns to laksa mixture

prawn laksa

PREPARATION TIME 35 MINUTES • COOKING TIME 40 MINUTES

1kg medium uncooked prawns
1/3 cup laksa paste (90g)
2 1/4 cups canned coconut milk (560ml)
1.25 litres chicken stock (5 cups)
2 red Thai chillies, seeded, chopped finely
1/4 cup lime juice (60ml)
1 tablespoon brown sugar
6 fresh Vietnamese mint leaves, torn
250g dried rice noodles
vegetable oil, for shallow-frying
300g fresh firm tofu, cut into 2cm cubes
200g bean sprouts
2 green onions, chopped finely

1 Shell and devein prawns, leaving tails intact.

2 Heat large dry saucepan; cook paste, stirring, until fragrant. Stir in milk, stock, chilli, juice, sugar and leaves. Bring to boil; simmer, covered, 30 minutes.

3 Meanwhile, cook noodles in large saucepan of boiling water, uncovered, until just tender; drain. Heat oil in wok or large heavy-base frying pan; cook tofu, in batches, until browned all over. Drain on absorbent paper.

4 Add prawns to laksa mixture; simmer, uncovered, about 5 minutes or until prawns are just changed in colour.

5 Just before serving, add noodles, tofu, sprouts and onion to pan; stir gently just until ingredients are combined and laksa is hot.

SERVES 4

per serve 46.3g fat; 3159kJ

tips

- This spicy Malaysian noodle soup is so popular you'll be rapt when you learn how to make it yourself – a lot of the work has been taken out of it thanks to the availability of commercially made laksa pastes, and the paste from the supermarket is just as pungently fragrant as the homemade.
- Don't seed the chillies if you like your laksa hot, or serve it, as they do in Malaysia, with a bowl of sambal oelek.
- Vietnamese mint, available from selected greengrocers and Asian food stores, is called by many different names – hot mint, Cambodian mint and daun laksa, which translates as laksa leaves. This herb gives laksa its particularly unique sharp spicy flavour.
- Omit the prawns in this recipe and substitute chopped cooked chicken or, for a vegetarian version, chopped baby bok choy, spinach or cabbage.

combination noodle soup

PREPARATION TIME 15 MINUTES • COOKING TIME 30 MINUTES

Removing chicken from pan

Adding prawns to the hot stock

500g chicken breast fillets
2 litres chicken stock (8 cups), see recipe below
1 tablespoon light soy sauce
125g fresh thin wheat noodles
100g small cooked shelled prawns
200g Chinese barbecued pork, sliced thinly
100g bean sprouts
4 green onions, sliced

1 Poach the chicken by placing it in a large frying pan containing 1 litre (4 cups) boiling water; as soon as the water comes to the boil again, turn heat to low and gently simmer chicken, uncovered, about 15 minutes or until cooked through.

2 Remove chicken from pan using a slotted spoon; when cool enough to handle, slice chicken thinly.

3 Combine stock and soy sauce in large saucepan, cover; bring to boil.

4 Add noodles to boiling stock; using tongs or a large metal fork, immediately separate the strands. Reduce heat, add chicken, prawns, pork, sprouts and onion to pan; simmer soup until heated through.

5 Using metal tongs, lift noodles from soup; divide among serving bowls. Ladle remaining soup over noodles.

SERVES 4

per serve 11.6g fat; 1847kJ

chicken stock

Combining the stock ingredients

2kg chicken bones
2 medium brown onions (300g), chopped coarsely
2 trimmed sticks celery (150g), chopped coarsely
2 medium carrots (250g), chopped coarsely
3 bay leaves
2 teaspoons black peppercorns
5 litres water (20 cups)

1 Combine ingredients in large saucepan or small boiler; simmer, uncovered, 2 hours. Strain through muslin set inside a sieve placed over a large heatproof bowl.

MAKES 2.5 LITRES (10 CUPS)

per 100ml 0.1g fat; 89kJ

tips

- To tell if chicken is cooked all the way through, after the suggested 15 minutes poaching time, remove one piece of chicken to a saucer. Cut the piece at its thickest point: if the chicken is an even, white texture in the centre, it is cooked through.
- Slice the chicken when it is cool enough to handle, but still warm – you'll find it slices more easily and neatly. If you don't want to use it immediately, cover and refrigerate the chicken until required.

tips

- The classic choice of pasta for minestrone is always a short, fat tube – the sturdy shape holds up well when boiled with the other ingredients. Elbow macaroni, tiny shells or even a very short penne are all good varieties to try.
- This meal-in-a-bowl is best made with homemade beef stock (see page 116) but you can use a commercially prepared stock – just be careful adding seasonings, as packaged stocks can be very salty.
- Cabbage is the traditional leafy green vegetable used in minestrone, but a combination of any greens (chopped spinach, kale, silverbeet, savoy cabbage) is also delicious.

minestrone

PREPARATION TIME 20 MINUTES • COOKING TIME 45 MINUTES

Minestrone comes from the word minestra, *the first course of an Italian meal, and it has come to mean any chunky, rustic soup.*

1 tablespoon olive oil
4 bacon rashers, chopped coarsely
2 medium brown onions (300g), sliced thickly
2 cloves garlic, crushed
1 medium carrot (120g), chopped coarsely
2 small potatoes (240g), chopped coarsely
2 trimmed celery sticks (150g), chopped coarsely
1.5 litres beef stock (6 cups)
400g can whole peeled tomatoes
2 tablespoons tomato paste
1 cup macaroni (150g)
1/2 cup frozen peas (60g)
1 cup finely shredded cabbage (80g)
2 small zucchini (180g), chopped coarsely

1 Heat oil in large saucepan; cook bacon, onion, garlic, carrot, potato and celery, stirring, until onion is soft.

2 Add stock, undrained crushed tomatoes and paste; bring to boil. Simmer, covered, about 30 minutes or until vegetables are tender, stirring occasionally.

3 Add pasta, peas, cabbage and zucchini; boil, uncovered, about 10 minutes or until pasta is just tender.

SERVES 4

per serve 7.9g fat; 1372kJ

serving suggestions Don't forget to pass around a bowl of freshly grated parmesan cheese for diners to sprinkle over their soup. A crisp, hot loaf of ciabatta, sliced, is perfect for dipping in the soup.

Adding carrot to pan

Adding finely shredded cabbage to pan

Adding noodles to boiling water

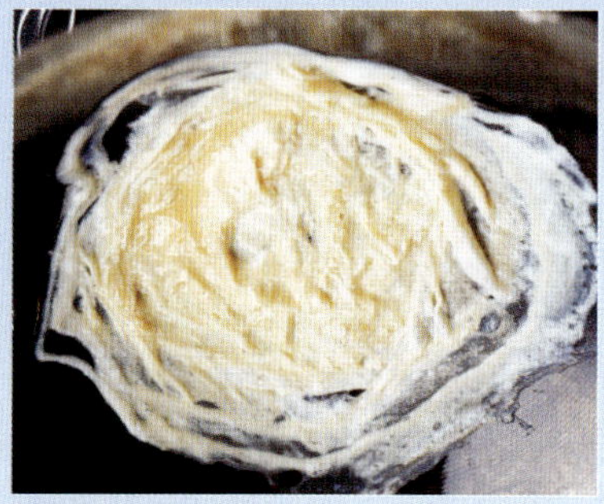
Swirling egg in wok to form omelette

Cutting rolled omelette into thin strips

singapore noodles

PREPARATION TIME 30 MINUTES • COOKING TIME 15 MINUTES

250g dried thin egg noodles
2 tablespoons peanut oil
4 eggs, beaten lightly
3 cloves garlic, crushed
1 tablespoon grated fresh ginger
1 medium white onion (150g), sliced thinly
2 tablespoons mild curry paste
230g can water chestnuts, drained, chopped coarsely
3 green onions, chopped on the diagonal
200g Chinese barbecued pork, sliced
500g medium uncooked prawns, shelled, deveined
2 tablespoons light soy sauce
2 tablespoons oyster sauce

1 Cook noodles in large saucepan of boiling water, uncovered, until just tender; drain.

2 Meanwhile, heat half of the oil in a hot wok or large heavy-base frying pan; add half of the egg, swirl wok to make a thin omelette. Remove omelette from wok; roll omelette, cut into thin strips. Repeat with remaining egg.

3 Heat remaining oil in wok; stir-fry garlic and ginger 1 minute. Add white onion and paste; stir-fry 2 minutes or until fragrant.

4 Add water chestnuts, green onion and pork; stir-fry about 2 minutes or until chestnuts are browned lightly.

5 Add prawns; stir-fry until prawns are just changed in colour. Add noodles, combined sauces and omelette; stir-fry, tossing, until sauce thickens and noodles are heated through.

SERVES 4

per serve 27.2g fat; 2658kJ

Quickly stir-frying ingredients

tips

- You can buy ready-to-eat barbecued pork at specialist Chinese barbecue shops.
- Have all the ingredients for this recipe chopped and ready to go so that they can be stir-fried in just a few minutes and eaten immediately – the noodles become unappetising and gluey after being mixed with the other ingredients if the finished dish sits for any length of time after the wok comes off the heat.

tips

- Vietnamese fish sauce is labelled as nuoc naam; the Thai version, naam pla, is almost identical.
- For a non-vegetarian variation, replace the cabbage with 16 medium cooked prawns.
- Any small red chillies can be used if you cannot find the Thai variety. If you want to increase the heat in the dipping sauce even further, don't seed the chillies. If you do seed the chillies, wear disposable kitchen gloves to do so – the seeds and membranes of these chillies can burn your skin.

vietnamese rice-paper spring rolls

PREPARATION TIME 40 MINUTES • STANDING TIME 25 MINUTES

Try to use authentic ingredients for this recipe – you'll find most of them in specialist greengrocers and Asian supermarkets.

6 dried shiitake mushrooms
50g thin rice stick noodles
1 Lebanese cucumber (130g)
8 sheets round rice paper
16 fresh Vietnamese mint leaves
1 medium carrot (120g), grated finely
$1\frac{1}{4}$ cups finely shredded cabbage (100g)
8 garlic chives
1 tablespoon rice vinegar
$\frac{1}{4}$ cup lime juice (60ml)
1 clove garlic, crushed
1 tablespoon sugar
$\frac{1}{4}$ cup fish sauce (60ml)
2 red Thai chillies, seeded, sliced thinly

1 Place mushrooms in small heatproof bowl, cover with boiling water; stand 20 minutes. Drain mushrooms; discard stems, chop caps finely.

2 Meanwhile, place noodles in medium heatproof bowl, cover with boiling water; stand until just tender. Drain noodles, pat dry with absorbent paper; cut noodles into 8 portions.

3 Halve unpeeled cucumber lengthways; discard seeds. Cut cucumber pieces in half crossways then into four strips lengthways.

4 Place 1 rice paper sheet in same medium heatproof bowl of warm water for about 1 minute or until softened slightly. Lift sheet from water, place on board; pat dry with absorbent paper. Repeat with remaining sheets.

5 Top each sheet with equal amounts of mushroom, noodle, cucumber, mint, carrot and cabbage. Fold in sides of sheet; roll top to bottom to enclose filling. About midway through rolling each sheet, enclose 1 garlic chive, protruding about 5cm beyond edge of roll.

6 Serve rice-paper spring rolls with dipping sauce made of combined remaining ingredients.

SERVES 4

per serve 3g fat; 326kJ

Chopping caps of soaked dried mushrooms

Cutting the noodles into portions

Seeding the cucumber

Assembling the rice-paper spring rolls

pasta with basil pesto

PREPARATION TIME 20 MINUTES • COOKING TIME 10 MINUTES

$1\frac{1}{2}$ cups firmly packed fresh basil leaves
2 cloves garlic, peeled
$\frac{1}{3}$ cup toasted pine nuts (50g)
$\frac{3}{4}$ cup olive oil (180ml)
50g parmesan cheese, grated coarsely
500g pasta

1. Pull basil leaves from stems; discard stems. Rinse basil well with cold water, drain; pat completely dry with absorbent paper.
2. Blend or process basil, garlic and pine nuts with a little of the olive oil. When basil mixture is pureed, with motor operating, gradually pour in remaining oil.
3. Turn off blender; use rubber spatula to push pesto down sides of bowl. Restart blender or processor; process, pausing, until mixture is well blended and smooth. Stir in cheese just before serving.
4. Cook pasta in large saucepan of boiling water, uncovered, until just tender; drain. Add pesto to hot pasta; using salad servers or a pasta fork, toss until well combined, serve immediately.

SERVES 4

per serve 56.7g fat; 3979kJ

Toasting pine nuts in the oven

Pulling basil leaves from stems

tips

- You'll need one very large bunch of fresh basil for this recipe. If it's summer and basil is in season, why not double or even quadruple the amounts of basil, garlic, pine nuts and olive oil, and freeze enough to see you through winter?
- Lash out and use extra virgin olive oil in this recipe.
- Add the parmesan to the made-ahead pesto base just before serving.
- Use 500g of whichever pasta you like, but remember that pesto clings well to the porous expanse of a strand of fettuccine or any "ribbon" pasta.

coriander and pecan pesto

Here's a non-traditional, very "today" pesto. Experiment at home, processing different pairs of various herbs and nuts – you may discover one combination that really delights you and your family.

Blend or process 1/2 cup chopped toasted pecans (60g), 2 peeled garlic cloves, 3/4 cup firmly packed fresh coriander leaves, coarsely chopped, and 2 tablespoons coarsely chopped fresh coriander root with 3/4 cup olive oil (180ml), following processing instructions for basil pesto, on opposite page. Serve with 500g hot pasta.

SERVES 4

per serve 55.5g fat; 3867kJ

fried rice

PREPARATION TIME 25 MINUTES • COOKING TIME 25 MINUTES

This dish is better if the rice is cooked the day before you intend to serve the fried rice – it was originally created as a means to use up yesterday's leftover rice. Because the rice grains are distinctly separate and cold, they do not stick together in an unpalatable mass when fast-fried with the remaining ingredients. Cook 1 cup (200g) of long-grain white rice by boiling it, uncovered, in a large saucepan of water until the rice is just tender. Drain rice then spread it on tray, cover with absorbent paper; refrigerate overnight.

tips

- Don't regard fried rice as just a way to use up assorted leftovers – prepared correctly, using specific, high-quality ingredients, this fried rice is a dish significant enough to serve as a main course on its own.
- You can freeze leftover rice in 1- or 2-cup portions, then thaw only the amount you need at any given time.

2 teaspoons peanut oil
2 eggs, beaten lightly
1 teaspoon sesame oil
4 bacon rashers, chopped coarsely
1 medium brown onion (150g), chopped coarsely
2 trimmed sticks celery (150g), sliced thickly
1 clove garlic, crushed
1 tablespoon grated fresh ginger
3 cups cold cooked long-grain white rice
100g small cooked shelled prawns
425g can baby corn, drained, sliced
1/2 cup frozen peas (125g), thawed
4 green onions, sliced thinly
1 tablespoon soy sauce

1 Heat one teaspoon of the peanut oil in a hot wok or large heavy-base frying pan; add half of the egg, swirl wok to make a thin omelette. Remove omelette from wok; roll omelette, cut into thin strips. Repeat with remaining egg.

2 Heat remaining peanut oil and sesame oil in same wok; stir-fry bacon until brown. Add onion, celery, garlic and ginger; stir-fry over high heat until vegetables are just tender.

3 Add rice, omelette and remaining ingredients to wok; stir-fry, tossing, until well combined and heated through.

SERVES 4

per serve 10.8g fat; 1586kJ

Spreading rice in a thin layer to cool

Swirling egg in wok to make omelette

Adding vegetables to wok

chicken

for your information...

A simple way to test if poached chicken is cooked through is to remove a piece of chicken from the saucepan and cut through to its centre, at its thickest point. If the meat has an even, white texture, it is done; if you detect any pink, uncooked meat, return the chicken (and any juices) to the pan for further cooking. Warm cooked chicken slices far more easily than cooled chicken.

No matter what chicken cut you use, if the skin is left on, the fat count of the recipe increases considerably.

Chicken shrinks during cooking, so cut it a little larger than the size you require for what you're making.

Thigh fillets are well suited to casseroles: their darker meat has more flavour and their slightly higher fat content helps them remain moist through long cooking times. Other chicken cuts can be used successfully in casseroles, but cooking times may change: breast fillets can be substituted for thigh fillets with no change to the cooking time, provided they are chopped the same way; tenderloins, uncut, will actually require less time; and chicken cuts with the bone in, such as whole thighs or thigh cutlets, need more time to cook.

perfect roast chicken

PREPARATION TIME 30 MINUTES • COOKING TIME 1 HOUR 30 MINUTES

We've given a traditional roast chicken recipe a Thai twist by using fresh coriander, kaffir lime leaves and lemon grass to flavour it instead of more commonly used seasonings.

1.5kg fresh chicken
1 bunch fresh coriander (about 100g), roots intact
4 kaffir lime leaves, torn
2 sticks lemon grass, chopped coarsely
2 kaffir limes, quartered
cooking-oil spray
1 teaspoon salt

1. Preheat oven to moderately hot. Wash cavity of chicken under cold water; pat dry with absorbent paper.
2. Wash coriander under cold water, removing any dirt clinging to the roots. Chop coriander roots, stems and leaves; place all of the coriander, the lime leaves and lemon grass, and 4 of the lime quarters inside the chicken cavity.
3. Tuck wings under chicken; trim skin around chicken neck, secure to underside of chicken with toothpicks or poultry pins. Tie legs together loosely using kitchen string.
4. Place chicken, breast-side up, on rack inside large baking dish. Spray chicken all over with cooking-oil spray; sprinkle with salt.
5. Place enough water in baking dish to come to a 1cm depth. Roast chicken, uncovered, in moderately hot oven for 1½ hours; cover loosely with foil after an hour if chicken starts to overbrown.
6. Discard toothpicks, kitchen string and cavity filling. Serve chicken, carved or cut into pieces, with remaining lime quarters.

SERVES 4

per serve 28.6g fat; 1746kJ

serving suggestions Continuing the Asian theme, accompany the chicken with steamed rice, and baby bok choy stir-fried with garlic and ginger.

Chopped herbs, kaffir limes and leaves

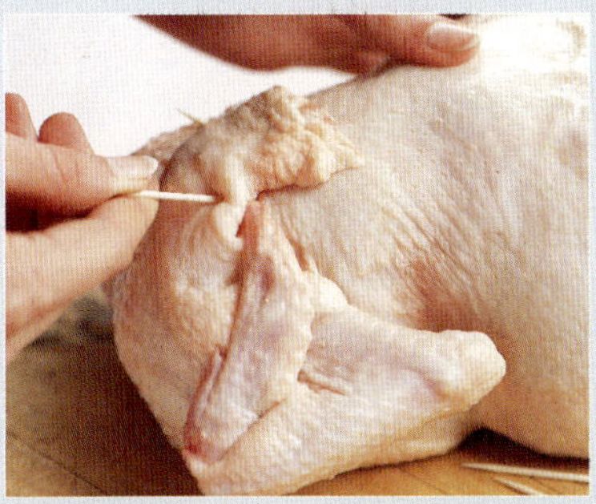

Securing the neck skin with toothpicks

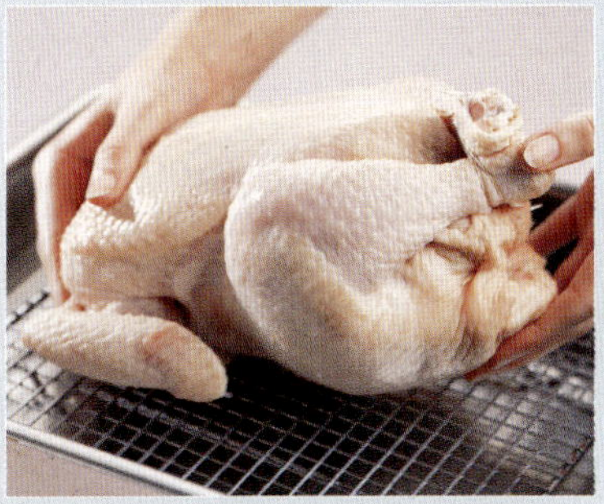

Placing chicken on rack inside baking dish

tips

- Use a plump, high-quality fresh chicken; experiment with free-range or corn- or barley-fed chickens.
- Fresh kaffir limes and leaves, lemon grass and coriander are available in greengrocers and many supermarkets. Substitute fresh lemon leaves, washed, for kaffir lime leaves; lemons or limes for kaffir limes; and strips of lemon or lime rind for the lemon grass.
- To test if the chicken is cooked, prick the thigh flesh where it meets the body with a metal skewer; if the juice that runs out is clear, it's done.

chicken à la provençale

PREPARATION TIME 20 MINUTES • COOKING TIME 45 MINUTES

We used a commercially made tomato-based pasta sauce containing black olives and anchovies, the flavours of Provence, but feel free to experiment with the many varieties available at your supermarket until you find the one you like best.

Cooking the chicken in batches

Adding pasta sauce to chicken mixture

1kg chicken thigh fillets
2 tablespoons olive oil
1 medium brown onion (150g), chopped coarsely
2 cloves garlic, crushed
1/2 cup dry sherry (125ml)
500g bottled tomato pasta sauce
1/4 cup loosely packed fresh curly parsley sprigs
1/3 cup black olives (50g), seeded

1 Discard any skin or fat from chicken pieces; cut chicken into large bite-size (about 3cm) pieces.

2 Heat half of the oil in large frying pan; cook chicken, in batches, over high heat until chicken is browned all over, turning frequently. Drain on absorbent paper.

3 Heat remaining oil in same pan; cook onion and garlic, stirring, over medium heat about 5 minutes or until onion just softens. Return chicken to pan; stir in sherry and pasta sauce. Cover, bring to boil; simmer, covered, about 20 minutes or until chicken is tender and cooked through.

4 Meanwhile, chop parsley sprigs finely.

5 Uncover chicken mixture; cook about another 10 minutes or until sauce just thickens. Stir in parsley and olives; serve immediately.

SERVES 4

per serve 21.7g fat; 2097kJ

serving suggestions Chicken à la Provençale can be served with pasta or fresh bread, and a mixed green salad (see page 96) or steamed vegetables.

tips

- To keep the chicken succulent and juicy, brown it in four batches. Too much cooked at once will reduce the heat in the frying pan and stew (thus toughen) the meat. Don't worry when browning chicken that it is not cooked all the way through – it shouldn't be at this stage.
- Use a large frying pan having its own tight-fitting lid in order to avoid the sauce becoming too thick, too fast.
- It won't be as authentic, but you can use vegetable oil in place of olive oil. Dry sherry can be substituted with dry red wine or the same amount of chicken stock.
- You can prepare this recipe ahead to the end of step 3. Cool chicken mixture for 10 minutes, place in a storage container; cover, refrigerate while still hot. To freeze, refrigerate mixture as above until cold; place in freezer.

chicken satay with jasmine rice

PREPARATION TIME 20 MINUTES (plus marinating time)
COOKING TIME 25 MINUTES

This is a good recipe to make for a crowd. Allowing 3 skewers per person, increase the amounts below proportionately according to the number of people you intend to feed. The marinated chicken can be skewered and frozen, tightly sealed, then thawed in the refrigerator the night before you want to cook it.

Coating chicken pieces with satay marinade

750g chicken thigh fillets
3/4 cup crunchy peanut butter (200g)
2/3 cup chicken stock (160ml)
2 tablespoons honey
2 tablespoons soy sauce
1 tablespoon Thai red curry paste
1 tablespoon lemon juice
2 cups jasmine rice (400g)
1 cup coconut milk (250ml)

Combining coconut milk and marinade

1 Cut chicken into 2cm pieces; combine in large bowl containing blended peanut butter, stock, honey, soy sauce, curry paste and lemon juice. Mix well to coat chicken in the marinade, cover; refrigerate 1 hour or overnight.

2 Just before serving, rinse rice in large strainer under cold water until water runs clear. Place rice in large saucepan containing 3 cups (750ml) boiling water; stir until water returns to the boil then cover pan with tight-fitting lid. Simmer rice 15 minutes, without lifting lid. Stand rice in pan, covered, 5 minutes.

Placing skewers on a foil-lined tray

3 Meanwhile, remove chicken from marinade; reserve marinade. Thread chicken on 12 bamboo skewers; place skewers, in single layer, on foil-lined oven tray. Cook under hot grill about 4 minutes each side or until browned and cooked through.

4 While skewers are cooking, place reserved marinade in small saucepan with coconut milk; bring to boil then cook, stirring, 5 minutes.

5 Serve skewers, rice and satay sauce separately.

SERVES 4

per serve 44.6 fat; 4271kJ

serving suggestions Accompany the skewers and rice with stir-fried or steamed Asian vegetables, like bok choy, snake beans or snow peas. Fresh cucumber slivers also go well with the flavour of satay.

tips

- Soak the bamboo skewers in water for at least an hour to avoid them burning when the chicken is grilled; this also helps prevent splinters when threading the chicken onto the skewers.
- "Dress-up" the marinade: add finely chopped lemon grass, fresh coriander and a red Thai chilli or two to the other ingredients. Similarly, stir some finely chopped coriander or spring onion through the cooked rice just before serving.
- It is vital to boil the satay sauce for 5 minutes – the marinade that forms its basis will contain raw chicken juice.
- Jasmine rice is well-suited to Asian recipes like this; however, you can use any white rice that you have on hand.

tips

- You can make your own chicken stock (see page 30) or you can use one of the commercially prepared versions available in supermarkets. If you prefer, you can use vegetable stock instead – try making it with the addition of a chopped stem of lemon grass for a delicious flavour.
- Try using different fresh noodles in this recipe – Hokkien, stir-fry or rice – but be sure to check the manufacturer's instructions regarding their preparation.
- It is important that the wok or frying pan you use is heated first so that it is quite hot by the time you add the oil. This keeps the chicken from "stewing" and becoming tough. Stir-frying the chicken in batches also keeps the wok as hot as possible and prevents the chicken from losing valuable juices and becoming chewy. Cooking "in batches" also indicates that the chicken is removed from the wok when it is just browned; further final cooking will take place when you return it to the wok later in the recipe.
- The fresh coriander is added off the heat just before serving the chicken; the leaves should be just wilted, not cooked.

lemon chicken

PREPARATION TIME 20 MINUTES (plus marinating time)
COOKING TIME 25 MINUTES

Almost everyone loves lemon chicken, so we've come up with this clever and delicious recipe for you to re-create at home for an appreciative audience. If you'd prefer, you can leave out the noodles and serve the lemon chicken stir-fry with plain white rice.

700g chicken breast fillets
1/3 cup lemon juice (80ml)
1 tablespoon brown sugar
1 tablespoon grated fresh ginger
2 cloves garlic, crushed
2 tablespoons peanut oil
250g dried thin egg noodles
1 medium brown onion (150g), sliced thinly
1 medium red capsicum (200g), sliced thinly
1 trimmed celery stick (75g), sliced thinly
4 green onions, sliced thinly
1/3 cup firmly packed fresh coriander leaves

LEMON SAUCE
1 teaspoon cornflour
2 teaspoons finely grated lemon rind
1/3 cup lemon juice (80ml)
2 cups chicken stock (500ml)
1/4 cup honey (60ml)
1 teaspoon sambal oelek

1. Cut chicken into thin, even-size slices; combine in large bowl containing blended lemon juice, sugar, ginger, garlic and 1 tablespoon of the oil. Mix well to coat chicken in the marinade, cover; refrigerate 1 hour or overnight.
2. Just before serving, cook noodles in large saucepan of boiling water, uncovered, until just tender. Drain in a large strainer.
3. Add remaining oil to a heated wok or large frying pan; stir-fry chicken mixture, in batches, until browned and almost cooked through. Add brown onion, capsicum, celery and green onion to same wok; stir-fry over high heat until vegetables are just browned.
4. Return chicken mixture to wok, add lemon sauce and noodles; stir-fry over high heat, tossing, until the sauce mixture just boils and thickens slightly. Stir in coriander leaves, off the heat, just before serving.

lemon sauce Blend cornflour with lemon rind and a little of the lemon juice by whisking them together in a small bowl or jug until smooth; stir in remaining juice, stock, honey and sambal, whisk to combine.

SERVES 4

per serve 19.7g fat; 2901kJ

Cutting the chicken into thin slices

Adding noodles to boiling water

Stir-frying the vegetables

Blending cornflour with lemon juice

vietnamese chicken salad

PREPARATION TIME 45 MINUTES • COOKING TIME 15 MINUTES

This salad is a perfect main course for a hot summer's night, accompanied by crisp deep-fried prawn crackers. Called krapuk, these are sold uncooked and packaged in large numbers; cook them as you do pappadums (see page 70). You will need a bunch of Vietnamese mint and a bunch of coriander for this recipe.

Poaching the chicken

Slicing the chicken pieces

Grated carrots and other ingredients

500g chicken breast fillets
1/4 cup peanut oil (60ml)
1/4 cup rice vinegar (60ml)
2 teaspoons fish sauce
1 teaspoon finely grated lime rind
1/4 cup lime juice (60ml)
2 small red Thai chillies, seeded, chopped finely
2 cloves garlic, crushed
2 tablespoons brown sugar
1/2 cup firmly packed, coarsely shredded fresh Vietnamese mint leaves
1/2 cup firmly packed, coarsely shredded fresh coriander leaves
500g finely shredded Chinese cabbage
2 medium (240g) carrots, grated coarsely
6 green onions, sliced thinly
1/3 cup coarsely chopped roasted unsalted peanuts (35g)

1 Poach the chicken by placing it in a medium frying pan containing 1 litre (4 cups) boiling water; as soon as the water returns to a boil, turn heat to low and gently simmer, uncovered, about 15 minutes or until chicken is cooked through.

2 Pour chicken into a large strainer placed over a large heatproof bowl; reserve poaching liquid for another use. When cool enough to handle, slice chicken.

3 Combine oil, vinegar, fish sauce, rind and juice in large bowl with chilli, garlic and sugar; stir until sugar is completely dissolved. Add all of the mint and about two-thirds of the coriander to the dressing mixture; toss gently to combine.

4 Add chicken slices, cabbage and carrot to the dressing mixture; toss gently to combine. Divide salad among serving bowls; sprinkle servings with equal amounts of remaining coriander, green onion and peanuts.

SERVES 4

per serve 23.3g fat; 1968kJ

tips

- If you're in a hurry, buy a barbecued chicken, discard the skin and bones, and slice the chicken meat.
- Use the poaching liquid from the chicken – freeze it if you don't have a use for it within a day or two – in place of water for cooking rice or other grains; for thinning a gravy; as a substitute for wine in a cooked sauce like a bolognese; or for using as the cooking liquid for any vegetables you intend to serve with this salad.
- Poaching and slicing the chicken is the only part of the recipe you can complete ahead of time.
- Vietnamese fish sauce is sometimes called just nuoc naam on the label; the Thai version, naam pla, is almost identical. Any small red chillies can be used in place of Thai chillies – and if you want to increase the heat even further, don't seed the chillies. If you do seed the chillies, do so wearing disposable kitchen gloves – the seeds and membranes of these chillies can burn your skin. If you prefer, substitute a teaspoon or two of sambal oelek for the fresh chillies.
- Use care when you grate the lime rind so that none of the bitter white pith goes into the dressing.

meat

for your information...

To prevent staining plastic storage containers (and avoid impregnating them with food flavours), use a non-reactive container, such as glass, when marinating meat. Make sure the meat is totally covered or coated with the marinade, then cover the container tightly with plastic wrap before refrigerating.

To avoid toughening meat, never turn it more than once during cooking.

To stand cooked meat, place it on a plate and cover it tightly with foil: let meat stand for the same length of time it's been cooked (although roasts need only stand 10 to 15 minutes). Standing allows the meat to "relax" and the juices to "settle", making slicing easier.

When a recipe calls for cooking meat in batches, make sure both the pan and the oil in it remain hot between batches – if the pan and oil are too cold, the meat will stew instead of seal, and the juices and flavour will be lost. Adding too much meat per batch also reduces the temperature of the pan, to similar effect. When cooking in batches, the meat will be browned but not cooked through; the cooking is completed further along in the recipe.

stir-fried pork and noodles

PREPARATION TIME 30 MINUTES • COOKING TIME 10 MINUTES

Because the cooking time is so brief in a stir-fry, it's best to use a cut of meat that doesn't need to be slow-cooked in order to be tender; we recommend you use thinly sliced pork fillet or rump in this recipe.

450g fresh egg noodles
1 tablespoon peanut oil
1 clove garlic, crushed
1½ teaspoons five-spice powder
500g pork fillet, sliced thinly
2 small red capsicums (300g), sliced diagonally
2 tablespoons oyster sauce
1 tablespoon soy sauce
2 teaspoons sesame oil
2 teaspoons cornflour
1⅓ cups chicken stock (330ml)
5 green onions, sliced thinly
600g Chinese cabbage, shredded

Slicing the pork against the grain

1 Place noodles in a large heatproof bowl; cover with boiling water, stand for 3 minutes, using a fork to separate the noodles. Drain into a colander or large strainer; reserve.

2 Add half of the peanut oil to a heated wok or large frying pan; stir-fry garlic and five-spice briefly, until just fragrant. Add pork, in batches, to wok; stir-fry over high heat until browned and almost cooked through.

3 Heat remaining peanut oil in wok; stir-fry capsicum for 1 minute.

4 Return pork to wok; add oyster sauce, soy sauce, sesame oil and the blended cornflour and chicken stock. Stir-fry over high heat, tossing, until the pork mixture just starts to boil and is thickened slightly.

5 Add noodles, onion and cabbage to wok; stir-fry over high heat, tossing to combine, until heated through.

SERVES 4

per serve 10.3g fat; 1699kJ

tips

- Use any fresh Asian noodle you like in this recipe – Hokkien, stir-fry or rice – but check the manufacturer's instructions regarding preparation.
- Garlic burns very easily so it's important to keep stir-frying time as brief as possible.
- Substitute a tablespoon of hoisin sauce for the five-spice powder for a different taste; just stir the garlic and hoisin together in the heated wok for a second or two before adding pork. Similarly, reduce the amount of sesame oil (or omit it) if you don't like it – or if you're watching your fat intake.
- To blend cornflour with the stock, put the measured amount of cornflour in a jug; using a teaspoon, gradually stir the stock into the cornflour. The mixture will become smooth and runny.

Cutting capsicum on the diagonal

Using a heavy knife to shred cabbage

veal campagnola

PREPARATION TIME 25 MINUTES • COOKING TIME 10 MINUTES

Some butchers sell veal steaks already pounded into appropriately thin scaloppine; if you purchase the meat this way, skip step 2 of this recipe. We used a 250g ball of processed mozzarella but you can substitute it with packaged grated pizza cheese or, even better, slices of fresh bocconcini. This rich meat dish is best accompanied with steamed rice or a plain boiled pasta, such as fettuccine, and a green salad dressed in balsamic vinegar and extra virgin olive oil.

300g spinach
4 veal steaks (500g)
1/4 cup plain flour (35g)
30g butter
1 tablespoon olive oil
500ml bottled tomato pasta sauce
250g mozzarella cheese, sliced thickly

1 Remove and discard stems from spinach; rinse leaves under cold water to remove grit. Drain; rinse again. Place spinach in colander to allow excess water to drain away.

2 Place each steak between pieces of plastic wrap; pound evenly and firmly until steaks are of the same thickness. Discard plastic wrap.

3 Place flour in shallow cake pan. Toss steaks, 1 at a time, in the flour, making sure both sides are evenly coated; shake away excess flour. Place steaks, in single layer, on a chopping board or plate.

4 Place large frying pan (having a tight-fitting lid) over high heat; add butter. When butter starts to sizzle, add all the spinach; cover immediately, turn off heat. Stand spinach 3 minutes without lifting lid.

5 Return wilted spinach to colander to drain; wipe out pan with absorbent paper. Place pan over high heat, add oil; move and turn pan so oil covers the base evenly. Add steaks, 1 at a time; cook, uncovered, until browned both sides. Drain each steak on absorbent paper.

6 Add pasta sauce to same pan; bring to boil over high heat. Place steaks, in single layer, on top of the boiling sauce; top each steak with one-quarter of the drained spinach then top spinach with a slice of cheese. Cover with lid; let mixture simmer about 1 minute or until cheese melts.

7 Place cheese- and spinach-topped steaks on individual serving plates; spoon sauce around each steak.

SERVES 4

per serve 27g fat; 2142kJ

Coating veal steaks with flour

Adding spinach to frying pan

Cooking veal until browned both sides

Topping veal steaks with spinach and cheese

tips

- If you like to cook with salt and pepper, mix in a sprinkle or two of each to the flour; this is what is known as "seasoned flour".
- Heat the serving plates for this recipe in a moderately slow oven for 10 minutes.
- Baby spinach leaves could be used in this recipe; they don't need trimming nor do they require such thorough washing.
- Because veal is low in fat, it has to be cooked quickly (overcooking will make it tough). This is the reason it is pounded to a uniform thickness. For the same reason, do not turn steaks more than once.

Removing leaves of herbs from stalks

tips

- For authenticity, we cooked our beef to medium-rare. To avoid toughening the beef, never turn it more than once during cooking.
- Substitute white onions with purple shallots (available seasonally from some greengrocers) or spring onions.
- If you don't have a blender or processor, finely chop chillies, lemon grass and coriander for the dressing then combine them with crushed garlic and remaining ingredients in a screw-top jar and shake well. The dressing can be made a day ahead and kept, covered, in the refrigerator.
- Assemble the salad close to serving. The beef should be warm and the vegetables and herbs still crisp.

Feeling resistance to test if beef is cooked

Seeding the cucumber

Slicing cooked beef across the grain

thai beef salad

PREPARATION TIME 25 MINUTES
COOKING TIME 7 MINUTES (plus standing time)

Unless you have access to homegrown herbs, you'll need to buy one bunch of fresh Thai basil, two bunches of fresh coriander, one bunch of fresh Vietnamese mint and two sticks of fresh lemon grass for this recipe.

400g beef rump steak
2 small white onions (160g)
2 Lebanese cucumbers (260g)
250g cherry tomatoes
1 large red Thai chilli, seeded, sliced thinly
1/4 cup loosely packed fresh Thai basil leaves
1/4 cup loosely packed fresh coriander leaves
1/4 cup loosely packed fresh Vietnamese mint leaves

GARLIC DRESSING
2 large red Thai chillies, seeded, chopped coarsely
2 tablespoons coarsely chopped fresh lemon grass
2/3 cup loosely packed fresh coriander leaves
3 cloves garlic, quartered
1/3 cup lime juice (80ml)
1 tablespoon fish sauce
1 tablespoon soy sauce

1 Cook beef on heated oiled grill plate (or grill or barbecue) until browned both sides and cooked as desired (about 5 to 10 minutes, depending on how well done you like your beef). Stand beef, covered, 5 to 10 minutes.

2 Meanwhile, slice onions thinly. Halve unpeeled cucumbers lengthways; scoop out seeds with a spoon, slice thinly. Halve tomatoes. Combine onion, cucumber, tomato, chilli and herbs in large bowl.

3 Slice beef thinly across the grain; add beef and garlic dressing to bowl, toss salad gently to combine.

garlic dressing Blend or process ingredients until finely chopped.

SERVES 4

per serve 7g fat; 800kJ

serving suggestions Serve Thai beef salad as part of a multi-course Asian banquet, or as the main dish of a light meal.

boeuf bourguignonne

PREPARATION TIME 35 MINUTES • COOKING TIME 2 HOURS 30 MINUTES

If you make your own beef stock (see page 116), this version of the French classic will be even more authentically flavoursome. Making this casserole ahead and refrigerating it, covered, overnight, will also enrich its full, homely flavour.

Trimming root end of onions

Stripping oregano leaves off stems

Browning beef in batches

1kg beef chuck steak
8 baby onions (200g)
3 bacon rashers
300g button mushrooms
1 tablespoon olive oil
30g butter
1 clove garlic, crushed
¼ cup plain flour (35g)
1 cup beef stock (250ml)
1 cup dry red wine (250ml)
2 bay leaves
1 tablespoon brown sugar
2 tablespoons finely chopped fresh oregano

1 Cut away and discard as much fat as possible from beef; cut into 3cm pieces. Peel onions, leaving root end trimmed but intact so onion remains whole during cooking. Cut off and discard rind from bacon; coarsely chop bacon. Trim mushroom stems.

2 Heat oil in large heavy-base flameproof casserole dish; cook beef, in batches, stirring, until browned all over.

3 Heat butter in same dish; cook onions, bacon, mushrooms and garlic over medium-high heat, stirring constantly, until onions are browned all over.

4 Sprinkle flour over onion mixture; cook, stirring, until flour is browned lightly. Remove dish from heat; gradually stir in stock, then wine.

5 Return dish to heat; cook, stirring, until mixture boils and thickens. Return beef with any juices to dish, add bay leaves and sugar; bring to boil. Simmer, covered, about 2 hours or until beef is tender, stirring every 30 minutes.

6 Discard bay leaves; stir in about half of the oregano, scattering the remainder over each portion just before serving.

SERVES 4

per serve 24.5g fat; 2408kJ

serving suggestions The French would accompany this rich and satisfying main dish with a fresh long loaf of crusty bread and a big bowl of greens just plucked from the garden, dressed simply with oil and vinegar, but we rather like it served with plain boiled noodles or mashed potatoes.

tips

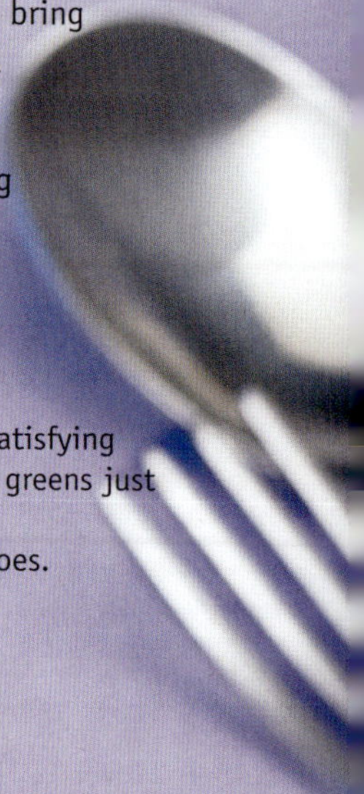

- Round, skirt or gravy beef (boned shin) can be used in place of the chuck steak.
- There's no need to peel the mushrooms. Simply wipe over the caps with a wet cloth or damp absorbent paper to remove any dirt.
- Make sure the butter is melted and hot, but not burning, before adding the onions, bacon, mushrooms and garlic.
- If you haven't the time to make your own stock, use a commercially prepared version or pour 1 cup of boiling water into a heatproof bowl and stir in either 1 crumbled stock cube or 1 teaspoon stock powder. As packaged stock is very salty, season this recipe with salt and pepper only after the stock has been added.
- The dish you use should have a tight-fitting lid so the casserole's liquid doesn't evaporate, leaving the meat and vegetables scorched.
- The casserole should simmer *gently*; check every 30 minutes, turning down the heat if the casserole is bubbling too much. Simmer mats distribute heat evenly across the base of the dish – a great help with gas burners.

basic meat sauce

PREPARATION TIME 15 MINUTES • COOKING TIME 40 MINUTES

1 tablespoon olive oil
1 large brown onion (200g), chopped finely
1 clove garlic, crushed
500g minced beef
2 x 400g cans tomato pieces
1/3 cup tomato paste (80g)
1 1/2 teaspoons sugar
1 cup beef stock (250ml)

1. Heat oil in large saucepan; cook onion and garlic, stirring, until onion softens. Add mince; cook, stirring, over medium heat until meat is cooked through.
2. Add undrained tomatoes, paste, sugar and stock, bring to boil; simmer, uncovered, stirring occasionally, about 25 minutes or until most of the liquid has evaporated.

SERVES 4

per serve 18.9g fat; 1403kJ

tips

- You can freeze the prepared meat sauce in small portions, ready to defrost, heat and serve on toast at a moment's notice. Basic meat sauce can be frozen up to 2 months.
- If you have time, make your own beef stock (see page 116) – otherwise, use a commercially prepared tetra-packed version. If you like, you can substitute the stock with dry red wine.
- Use a white or red onion if you don't have a brown one.
- To add to the flavour, just before serving stir a tablespoon or two of finely chopped fresh basil or oregano into the bolognese sauce; or 2 teaspoons of ground cumin into the chile con carne.

chile con carne

PREPARATION TIME 5 MINUTES
COOKING TIME 10 MINUTES

420g can red kidney beans, rinsed, drained
3 red Thai chillies, seeded, chopped finely
1 quantity basic meat sauce

1 Combine beans, chilli and meat sauce in large saucepan, bring to boil; simmer, uncovered, about 5 minutes or until hot.

SERVES 4

per serve 19.5g fat; 1765kJ

serving suggestion Serve chile con carne with corn chips or toasted tortilla wedges, or wrap in warm corn tortillas and top with sour cream and mashed avocado.

tip Beans must be rinsed well to remove all trace of the canning liquid. A can of refried beans may be used in place of the red kidney beans, if desired.

spaghetti bolognese

PREPARATION TIME 2 MINUTES
COOKING TIME 10 MINUTES

500g spaghetti
1 quantity basic meat sauce
50g parmesan cheese

1 Cook spaghetti in large saucepan or small boiler of boiling water, uncovered, until just tender; drain.
2 Meanwhile, heat meat sauce until just boiling.
3 Using a vegetable peeler, flake cheese.
4 Serve spaghetti topped with meat sauce and cheese.

SERVES 4

per serve 24.3g fat; 3422kJ

Flaking cheese with vegetable peeler

nachos

PREPARATION TIME 15 MINUTES
COOKING TIME 30 MINUTES

Commercially prepared taco seasoning mix can be found in most supermarkets.

35g packet taco seasoning mix
1/2 quantity basic meat sauce
1 medium avocado (250g)
1 teaspoon Tabasco sauce
2 teaspoons lemon juice
230g packet plain corn chips
1 1/2 cups grated cheddar cheese (185g)
2/3 cup sour cream (160ml)

1 Combine seasoning mix with meat sauce in large saucepan, bring to boil; simmer, uncovered, 5 minutes.
2 Meanwhile, mash avocado with fork in small bowl; stir in Tabasco and juice.
3 Divide corn chips among four heatproof serving plates; top chips on each plate with 2 tablespoons of cheese, then one-quarter of meat sauce. Sprinkle remaining cheese evenly over the meat sauce on each plate; place one or two plates at a time under hot grill for about 5 minutes or until cheese melts. To serve, top nachos with avocado mixture and sour cream.

SERVES 4

per serve 67.8g fat; 3842kJ

tip Make the avocado mixture a few hours ahead, cover tightly; place in the refrigerator.

osso buco

PREPARATION TIME 20 MINUTES • COOKING TIME 1 HOUR 15 MINUTES

Butchers variously refer to this meat cut as "veal shin" or "osso buco"; as long as it's veal shin cut into 3cm- to 5cm-thick slices, you're on the right track. Osso buco, *when translated from Italian, actually means "bone with a hole", probably to draw attention to the fact that the cooked marrow confined within this "hole" is one of the most delicious things one will ever taste. This long-braised meat and vegetable dish is native to Lombardy, the region in north-central Italy where Milan is situated; osso buco is often served with a risotto milanese (see page 29). Here, we show it topping creamy, freshly made polenta.*

Peeling the tomato

1/4 cup plain flour
8 pieces veal shin or osso buco (approximately 1kg)
2 tablespoons olive oil
3 large egg tomatoes (270g), peeled, chopped coarsely
1/2 cup dry white wine (125ml)
2 cloves garlic, crushed
2 cups chicken stock

POLENTA

1.5 litres water (6 cups)
2 teaspoons salt
1 1/2 cups yellow cornmeal (250g)
1/2 cup milk (125ml)

GREMOLATA

1/4 cup finely chopped fresh flat-leaf parsley
2 teaspoons finely chopped lemon rind
2 cloves garlic, chopped finely

Coating veal with flour inside a plastic bag

Fitting the browned veal upright in pan

Covering osso buco with baking paper

tips

- Browning the meat properly is very important for the final colour and taste of osso buco. Make sure the oil is hot before adding veal to pan.
- When veal is fitted – upright, like wheels – into the pan after browning, it should be squeezed in tightly so there's no chance the marrow can escape into the pan liquid.
- The baking paper helps hold the veal in place and slow evaporation.
- Substitute a 400g can of undrained tomato pieces for the fresh tomato.
- Osso buco is one of those fortunate dishes that improves with overnight refrigeration, and it can be frozen with no loss of flavour or quality.

1 Place flour in a plastic bag then, if you like salt and pepper, add a sprinkle or two of each to bag. Add 1 piece of veal at a time, gently shaking the bag to coat veal all over. Remove veal from the bag, shaking off any excess flour; repeat with remaining veal pieces.

2 Preheat oven to moderately slow.

3 Heat oil in large ovenproof saucepan or casserole dish over high heat; move and turn pan so oil covers the base evenly. Cook veal, in batches, until browned and almost crunchy on both sides.

4 Return browned veal pieces to the same pan, fitting them upright and tightly together in a single layer. Add tomato, wine, garlic and stock; if necessary, add enough water so that the liquid just covers the surface of the veal. Bring to the boil then place a round piece of baking paper, cut to the same diameter as the pan, on top of the veal. Cover pan with a tight-fitting lid; cook veal mixture in moderately slow oven for 1½ hours.

5 After 1 hour, check the liquid content in pan; if it looks too thin, remove pan from oven and simmer, uncovered, on top of stove until mixture reduces and thickens slightly. Return pan to oven, covered, and cook the osso buco for 30 minutes. Make the polenta while osso buco cooks.

6 Divide polenta among serving plates; top with osso buco and sprinkle with gremolata.

polenta Combine the water and salt in a large saucepan over high heat. When the water boils, add the cornmeal in a slow, steady stream, stirring constantly; reduce heat to a simmer and cook polenta, uncovered, stirring constantly, about 20 minutes or until polenta is just thickened. Stir in milk; cook, stirring constantly, about 10 minutes or until polenta is thick and creamy.

gremolata Combine ingredients in small bowl; cover tightly with plastic wrap and refrigerate until required.

SERVES 4

per serve osso buco 13.3g fat; 1831kJ polenta 1.3g fat; 879kJ

gourmet steak sandwiches

PREPARATION TIME 5 MINUTES
(plus marinating time)
COOKING TIME 15 MINUTES

We've given you some suggestions for marinades opposite; mix and match until you find the combination of meat and marinade you like most. You might like to add a dollop of pesto to each sandwich – try our recipe on page 38 or use a commercially prepared variety – but be mindful of the extra grams of fat a spoonful of pesto will contribute.

8 slices white bread
1 tablespoon olive oil
4 small marinated meat pieces (400g)
1 quantity oven-roasted tomatoes, see recipe above right
1 quantity caramelised onion, see recipe opposite
100g mesclun

1 Brush both sides of bread with oil.

2 Cook meat on heated oiled grill plate (or grill or barbecue) until browned both sides and cooked as desired; cover to keep warm.

3 Cook bread, in batches, on heated oiled grill plate until browned both sides.

4 Sandwich meat, tomato, onion and mesclun between bread slices.

MAKES 4 SANDWICHES

per sandwich 38g fat; 2715kJ (based on 1 portion of beef in red wine marinade)

oven-roasted tomatoes

Cut 6 medium egg tomatoes (450g) in half; drizzle with 1 tablespoon olive oil in medium baking dish; bake, uncovered, in hot oven about 30 minutes or until tomato is tender and browned lightly.
Serves 4. Per serve: 4.9g fat; 239kJ.

tips Any type of tomato may be used in this recipe. Try the vine-ripened or hydroponically grown varieties.

• Roast the tomatoes in a baking dish having deep sides; this shields them from the heat, so as not to burn.

caramelised onion

Heat 60g butter in large frying pan; cook 4 thickly sliced medium red onions (680g) and 2 cloves crushed garlic, stirring, until onion is soft and browned lightly. Add 2 tablespoons brown sugar and 2 tablespoons balsamic vinegar; cook, stirring constantly, about 20 minutes or until onion is well browned and mixture thickened. Serves 4. Per serve: 13g fat; 788kJ.

tips If you don't have red onions, regular brown onions work just as well when caramelising.

- Red wine or cider vinegar can be used in place of balsamic vinegar.
- If refrigerated, caramelised onion will solidify; reheating it gently and briefly will melt the butter and soften the onion.

tips

- Experiment with different kinds of bread – try pocket pitta, pide (Turkish bread), ciabatta or sourdough.
- Adjust the quantities of each sandwich's component parts to your own liking; for instance, you might prefer to use more oven-roasted tomato and less onion.
- Mesclun is a mixture of leaves from various greens (baby spinach, lettuces, rocket, etc) sold by weight in most greengrocers. You can substitute it with any single variety of lettuce if you prefer.
- Marinades not only add flavour to meat, they help tenderise it too.

marinades

Each quantity of the marinades below is sufficient for marinating 400g of meat. We like lamb eye of loin (ie, lamb backstrap) with the Greek marinade; beef fillet steaks with the red wine marinade; and pork with the balsamic vinegar marinade – but, by all means, try them with chicken and fish too.

balsamic vinegar marinade

Combine 1/2 cup balsamic vinegar (125ml), 1/4 cup olive oil (60ml), 1/3 cup firmly packed brown sugar (75g) and 1 tablespoon finely chopped fresh oregano in large shallow non-reactive bowl with 400g meat, fish or poultry pieces, cover; refrigerate 3 hours or overnight. Drain, discard marinade; cook meat as instructed in main recipe, or as desired.

greek marinade

Combine 1/2 cup lemon juice (125ml), 1/2 cup olive oil (125ml) and 1 tablespoon finely chopped fresh rosemary in large shallow non-reactive bowl with 400g meat, fish or poultry pieces, cover; refrigerate 3 hours or overnight. Drain, discard marinade; cook meat as instructed in main recipe, or as desired.

red wine marinade

Combine 1 cup dry red wine (250ml), 2 cloves crushed garlic, 1 tablespoon seeded mustard and 1/4 cup olive oil (60ml) in large shallow non-reactive bowl with 400g meat, fish or poultry pieces, cover; refrigerate 3 hours or overnight. Drain, discard marinade; cook meat as instructed in main recipe, or as desired.

tips

- You can use shanks that haven't been french-trimmed for this dish if you like, but the servings will be considerably larger and also have a higher fat count.
- If you haven't time to make beef stock (see recipe page 116), use the commercially prepared stock available in tetra packs from the supermarket. Use caution when seasoning this dish because packaged stock is quite salty.
- This recipe can be frozen with no loss of flavour or quality, although the couscous should be freshly made. Remember to remove and discard any surface fat that has accumulated after freezing before you reheat the lamb.

Chopping unpeeled onions, carrot and celery

Removing thyme leaves from stems

Browning lamb shanks all over

Fluffing couscous with a fork

braised lamb shanks with celery

PREPARATION TIME 15 MINUTES • COOKING TIME 1 HOUR 45 MINUTES

To "french" lamb cuts means to clean away the excess gristle, fat and meat from the end of a shank, cutlet or rack, to expose the bone. Ask your butcher to prepare the meat for you this way. While we've served the shanks with couscous, this homely dish also goes well with a mushroom risotto (see page 27). Steamed green vegetables also complement this rich meat dish.

2 tablespoons olive oil
500g trimmed celery (about 6 sticks), chopped coarsely
2 medium unpeeled brown onions (300g), chopped coarsely
2 cloves garlic, crushed
2 medium carrots (240g), chopped coarsely
4 french-trimmed lamb shanks (1kg)
3/4 cup dry white wine (180ml)
1/4 cup tomato paste (60g)
3 cups beef stock (750ml)
2 tablespoons fresh thyme leaves
1 1/2 cups beef stock (375ml), extra
1 1/2 cups couscous (300g)

1 Heat half of the oil in a large saucepan having a tight-fitting lid; cook celery, onion, garlic and carrot, stirring, until onion is soft. Remove vegetables from pan.

2 Heat remaining oil in same pan; cook shanks, uncovered, until browned all over. Stir in wine, tomato paste, stock and thyme, bring to a boil; simmer, covered, 1 hour. Return vegetables to pan; simmer, covered, about 30 minutes or until shanks are tender.

3 Just before serving, prepare the couscous. Heat the extra 1 1/2 cups of beef stock in a small saucepan over high heat; after stock boils, pour it over couscous in medium heatproof bowl. Stand couscous, covered, about 5 minutes or until stock is absorbed. Fluff couscous with fork and serve with lamb and vegetables.

SERVES 4

per serve 13.4g fat; 2462kJ

roast leg of lamb with gravy

PREPARATION TIME 10 MINUTES • COOKING TIME 2 HOURS

When you prepare this recipe, you'll understand why some people would give up a date with Tom Cruise rather than miss out on a home-cooked roast. Making a scrumptious roast is just a matter of following a few tried and tested rules and not trying to improve on perfect.

1 bunch fresh rosemary
2kg leg of lamb
2 cloves garlic, each cut into 8 slices
1/4 cup olive oil (60ml)
40g butter
1 small brown onion (80g), chopped finely
2 tablespoons plain flour
1/2 cup dry red wine (125ml)
1 1/2 cups lamb or beef stock (375ml)

1 Preheat oven to hot.

2 Cut 16 similar-size rosemary sprigs from bunch; place remainder of bunch in large flameproof baking dish.

3 Remove and discard as much excess fat from lamb as possible. Pierce surface of lamb all over, making 16 small cuts with a sharp knife; press garlic slices and rosemary sprigs into cuts.

4 Place lamb on top of rosemary in baking dish. Pour oil over the lamb; roast, uncovered, in hot oven 20 minutes. Reduce temperature to moderate; roast lamb, occasionally spooning pan juices over, another 1 1/2 hours. Remove lamb from pan; stand 5 minutes before slicing.

5 Drain juices from pan, melt butter in pan over low heat; cook onion, stirring, until soft. Stir in flour; cook, stirring, about 5 minutes or until browned. Pour in wine and stock; cook over high heat, stirring, until gravy boils and thickens. Strain gravy; serve with lamb.

SERVES 6

per serve 26.3g fat; 2038kJ

Studding lamb with garlic and rosemary

Spooning pan juices over lamb

Browning flour for gravy

tips

- Try substituting fresh lemon thyme, mint or flat-leaf parsley for the rosemary.
- Rest the roast, covered in foil, 10 to 15 minutes before carving so that the juices "settle". When carving the roast, slice across the grain – the meat is more tender this way.
- For the stock, make your own (substituting lamb bones for beef in our beef stock recipe on page 116), use a commercially prepared version or combine 1 cup of boiling water with 1 crumbled stock cube or 1 teaspoon stock powder.
- We used red shiraz in this recipe but any dry red wine can be used.
- The gravy recipe can easily be adapted into either a peppercorn or mushroom gravy. Return strained gravy to a clean saucepan then add either 1 tablespoon of drained, rinsed, canned green peppercorns or 100g finely sliced cooked button mushrooms to gravy. Cook, stirring, 2 minutes; serve.

lamb curry with cucumber raita

PREPARATION TIME 40 MINUTES • COOKING TIME 1 HOUR

The yogurt salad known as raita is a traditional accompaniment to many Indian meat and vegetable dishes. It works well as a partner to these spicy foods because it helps "cut" the richness of a strongly flavoured, thickly sauced curry. Yogurt and cucumber are two of the best antidotes for a chilli overdose, and when combined as they are in this recipe, they make a splendid neutraliser to be used in case of fire! Whatever you do, don't try to douse the flame in your mouth with a glassful of water – it dissipates the heat, rather than rinsing it away, and will not provide any relief.

Sprinkling salt over eggplant

Cooking lamb, in batches, until browned

Adding lentils to boiling water

1 medium eggplant (300g)
coarse cooking salt
1kg boned forequarter lamb, trimmed
2 medium potatoes (400g)
1 medium red capsicum (200g)
2 tablespoons vegetable oil
2 medium brown onions (300g), chopped coarsely
2 trimmed celery sticks (150g), chopped coarsely
2 cloves garlic, crushed
1 tablespoon grated fresh ginger
1/4 cup mild curry paste (70g)
425g can tomatoes
1 cup coconut milk (250ml)
1 1/2 cups brown lentils (300g)
vegetable oil, for deep-frying
12 pappadums

CUCUMBER RAITA

1 Lebanese cucumber (130g)
1 cup yogurt (250ml)
1 clove garlic, crushed

1 Cut unpeeled eggplant into 2cm cubes, place in colander, sprinkle all over with salt; stand 30 minutes to drain.

2 Meanwhile, cut lamb, potatoes and capsicum into 3cm pieces. Heat 1 tablespoon of the vegetable oil in large frying pan; cook lamb, in batches, until browned all over. Heat remaining oil in same pan; cook onion, celery, garlic, ginger and curry paste, stirring, until onion is soft.

3 Rinse eggplant well under cold water; pat dry with absorbent paper. Combine eggplant with onion mixture in pan; add undrained crushed tomatoes, potato, capsicum and the lamb, stir until curry mixture comes to a boil. Simmer, covered, about 30 minutes or until lamb is just tender.

4 After curry mixture has cooked for about 30 minutes, add coconut milk; simmer, uncovered, about a further 10 minutes or until sauce thickens slightly.

5 Meanwhile, add lentils to medium saucepan of boiling water; cook, uncovered, about 10 minutes or until just tender. Drain lentils; cover to keep warm.

6 Heat vegetable oil for deep-frying in large frying pan; cook pappadums, 1 at a time, until golden brown and puffed both sides, turning with metal tongs if necessary. Drain pappadums on absorbent paper.

7 Serve lamb curry with lentils, pappadums and raita, plus steamed white rice if desired.

cucumber raita Combine ingredients in small bowl.

SERVES 4

per serve 49.3g fat; 4431kJ

tips

- Salting and standing a chopped eggplant is called "disgorging": the eggplant's bitter juices are drawn out by the salt and washed away when you rinse off the salt.
- In place of a boned forequarter, you can use meat cut from a leg of lamb, backstrap or even eye of loin.
- Pappadums of many different flavours can be found, ready to be cooked. Re-wrap any you don't use in plastic wrap or seal in a plastic bag. They taste better deep-fried, but for a quick, low-fat alternative, "puff" the pappadums in a microwave oven. Just place two pappadums at a time directly on the turntable and cook them on HIGH (100%) for 30 seconds. Cooled puffed pappadums can be kept in an airtight storage container for a few days before going soggy.

roast rolled pork loin and crackling

PREPARATION TIME 30 MINUTES • COOKING TIME 2 HOURS

Ask your butcher to bone a loin of pork, leaving a flap large enough to stuff, roll and tie the meat easily. Get the butcher to leave on the rind and accompanying layer of fat – what's roast pork without crackling? We give you a choice of stuffings here – decide between the breadcrumb stuffing or the apricot, prune and rice stuffing before you start cooking so that you have all the necessary ingredients on hand. Serve the stuffed pork and crackling with traditional roast potatoes (see page 92) and steamed vegetables.

2.5kg loin of pork, with rind, boned
1 tablespoon olive oil
2 teaspoons sea salt
1 tablespoon plain flour
1½ cups chicken stock (375ml)

BREADCRUMB STUFFING

2 cups stale breadcrumbs (140g)
1 egg, beaten lightly
2 tablespoons finely chopped fresh flat-leaf parsley
2 tablespoons finely chopped fresh chives
2 tablespoons finely chopped fresh sage

APRICOT, PRUNE AND RICE STUFFING

⅔ cup white long-grain rice (130g)
½ cup finely chopped dried apricots (75g)
½ cup finely chopped seeded prunes (105g)

tips

- The pork rind is separated from the fatty layer so the right amount of fat is left attached to the rind to make the crackling crisp but not so hard you can't chew it. You'll find it easiest to cut the browned crackling into strips while it's still hot. Reheat the crackling by placing it, uncovered, in a very hot oven for a few minutes.
- You don't have to strain the gravy – if it's been stirred well throughout cooking, it should be relatively lump-free. However, if in doubt, it does no harm to pour the gravy through a fine strainer into its serving container.

Easing rind away from the pork

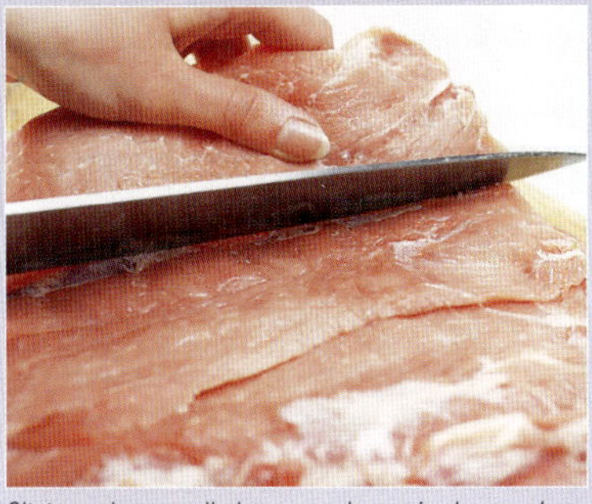
Slicing almost all the way through the pork

Pressing the stuffing up against the loin

1 Preheat oven to very hot.

2 Place pork on board, rind-side up. Run a sharp knife about 5mm under rind, between it and the meat, gradually lifting and easing rind away from pork. Place rind, right-side up, in large shallow flameproof baking dish. Score rind, making diagonal cuts; rub with half of the oil, sprinkle with salt. Bake in very hot oven, uncovered, about 40 minutes or until crackling is well browned and crisp. Chop crackling into serving pieces. Reduce oven temperature to hot.

3 Meanwhile, prepare your choice of stuffing. Place pork, fat-side down, on board. Slice through the thickest part of the meat horizontally, without cutting through at the side. Open out meat to form one large piece; press stuffing against the loin along width of pork. Roll pork to enclose stuffing, securing with kitchen string at 2cm intervals.

4 Place rolled pork in same baking dish, brush with remaining oil; roast, uncovered, in hot oven about 1 hour or until cooked through. Remove pork from baking dish; cover to keep warm while making the gravy.

5 Pour away and reserve all but 1 tablespoon of pan drippings from baking dish. Heat dripping in baking dish on top of the stove, stir in flour; cook, stirring, until mixture bubbles and is browned to your liking. Add reserved pan drippings and stock to pan gradually; cook, stirring, until gravy boils and thickens. Pour gravy into serving jug. Serve with pork and reheated crackling.

breadcrumb stuffing Combine ingredients in a large bowl.

apricot, prune and rice stuffing Cook rice in large pan of boiling water, uncovered, about 15 minutes or until just tender; drain. Combine cooled rice in large bowl with remaining ingredients.

SERVES 6

per serve pork, crackling and gravy 96.2g fat; 4894kJ breadcrumb stuffing 1.2g fat; 175kJ apricot, prune and rice stuffing 0.2g fat; 557kJ

Rolling pork firmly to enclose stuffing

for your information...

In recipes where the fish is to be coated with spices, tossed in flour or dipped in batter before cooking, selecting a dry fish (silver warehou, snapper, trevally, dhufish, etc) is recommended. Dry fish is less likely to lose its coating when it comes into contact with heat. For this reason, avoid using thawed frozen fish for such recipes.

Check over fish fillets and remove any remaining bone or skin – salting your fingers will help give you a better grip when pulling away the skin, and tweezers are ideal to pick out any bones.

thai-style fish cutlets

PREPARATION TIME 10 MINUTES • COOKING TIME 20 MINUTES

Shredding kaffir lime leaves

Finely chopping palm sugar

Pinching foil to seal fish parcels

4 blue-eye cutlets (800g)
4 green onions, sliced thinly
4 kaffir lime leaves, shredded thinly
80g fresh ginger, peeled, sliced thinly
1/4 cup coarsely chopped fresh coriander leaves
1/4 cup finely chopped palm sugar (65g)
2 tablespoons sweet chilli sauce
2 teaspoons peanut oil
1 teaspoon fish sauce
2 tablespoons lime juice

1 Preheat oven to moderate.

2 Place cutlets on individual large pieces of foil; top each cutlet with equal amounts of onion, lime leaf, ginger, coriander and sugar. Drizzle combined remaining ingredients over each serving then fold foil over the top, pinching it tightly to enclose cutlets.

3 Place fish parcels on oven tray; cook in moderate oven 20 minutes then test one parcel to see if fish is cooked as desired. If not, re-wrap sample piece and cook about 5 minutes longer or until the piece is done to your liking. Fish parcels can also be placed on pre-heated grill of covered barbecue and cooked about 10 minutes or until fish is cooked as desired.

SERVES 4

per serve 7.2g fat; 1171kJ

tips

- You can use any firm white fish for this recipe – try bream, sea perch, swordfish, tuna or whiting – but cooking times will alter.
- If you can, use banana leaves in place of the foil. Cut leaves into large squares then dip into boiling water. Rinse with cold water and dry thoroughly. Wrap each cutlet in a square of banana leaf so it is completely enclosed; cook as directed in recipe.
- You can substitute dark brown sugar for the palm sugar.

tips

- If you cannot find fresh Vietnamese mint, use whatever kind of mint is available. Buy fresh coriander with the roots intact: the roots are an ingredient.
- Vietnamese fish sauce is sometimes labelled nuoc naam; the Thai version, naam pla, is almost identical.
- Any small red chillies can be substituted for Thai chillies. We used a hot Vietnamese chilli paste here but you can use sambal oelek (chilli with ginger and garlic) or, for less heat, mild sweet Thai chilli sauce.
- Prawns are cooked when pink-orange in colour.
- You can buy fish stock in tetra packs from the supermarket, or canned or frozen from Asian food stores. Alternatively, you can easily make your own.

Deveining prawns

Slicing peeled ginger

Plucking coriander and mint leaves from stems

tom yum goong

PREPARATION TIME 30 MINUTES • COOKING TIME 20 MINUTES

This is probably the Thai soup most favoured by Westerners. Sour and tangy, tom yum goong can easily become a main meal by adding more prawns – say 3 per person – to the basic recipe. You will need about 2 medium limes for this recipe.

1.5 litres fish stock (6 cups), see recipe right
1 bunch fresh coriander
1 bunch fresh Vietnamese mint
1 stalk fresh lemon grass, chopped finely
4 fresh kaffir lime leaves, torn
40g fresh ginger, peeled, sliced thinly
4 small red Thai chillies, seeded, sliced thinly
1 tablespoon fish sauce
16 uncooked medium prawns (400g)
8 green onions
1/3 cup fresh lime juice (80ml)
1 teaspoon chilli paste

1 Heat stock, uncovered, in large saucepan.

2 Meanwhile, wash coriander and mint separately; shake to remove excess water. Cut off coriander roots, add to stock in pan; dry remaining coriander and mint on absorbent paper, reserve.

3 Add lemon grass, lime leaves, ginger, chilli and sauce to stock, bring to boil; simmer, uncovered, 10 minutes.

4 Meanwhile, shell and devein prawns, leaving heads and tails intact. Chop green onions into 2cm lengths. Pluck coriander and mint leaves from the stems; you need about 2/3 cup loosely packed coriander leaves and 1/2 cup loosely packed mint leaves.

5 Remove and discard coriander roots from stock mixture. Add prawns, green onion, lime juice and chilli paste to pan; simmer, uncovered, about 4 minutes or until prawns just change in colour. Add coriander and mint leaves; serve immediately.

SERVES 4

per serve 0.9g fat; 583kJ

fish stock

3 litres cold water (12 cups)
1.5kg fish trimmings (bones, heads, tails, etc)
2 bay leaves
1 teaspoon whole black peppercorns
1 medium brown onion (150g), chopped coarsely
2 untrimmed sticks celery (300g), chopped coarsely

1 Place cold water in large saucepan or small boiler over high heat. Add fish trimmings, bay leaves, peppercorns, onion and celery (if you like to cook with salt, add 2 teaspoons now), bring to boil; simmer, uncovered, 20 minutes.

2 Strain stock into colander or large metal sieve over large saucepan or heatproof bowl; discard all solids in colander. Stock is now ready to use and will keep, covered, in the refrigerator up to 3 days.

MAKES 21/2 litres (10 CUPS)

per litre 1g fat; 140kJ

octopus with seasoned salt

PREPARATION TIME 20 MINUTES • COOKING TIME 10 MINUTES

1kg baby octopus
2 cloves garlic, crushed
2 tablespoons peanut oil
2 teaspoons five-spice powder
2 teaspoons sea salt
4 kaffir lime leaves, shredded
1 small red Thai chilli, seeded, sliced thinly

1 Remove and discard heads and beaks from octopus; cut each octopus in half.

2 Combine octopus in large bowl with garlic, oil and five-spice, cover; refrigerate 3 hours or overnight.

3 Char-grill (or barbecue or pan-fry) undrained octopus, in batches, until browned all over and just cooked through.

4 Combine octopus in large bowl with remaining ingredients; toss gently to combine.

SERVES 4

per serve 12.2g fat; 1080kJ

Removing head and beak from octopus

char-grilled calamari salad

PREPARATION TIME 20 MINUTES (plus marinating time)
COOKING TIME 10 MINUTES

After squid are cleaned and cut into rings, they are often referred to as calamari; for this recipe, you can buy 750 grams calamari rings fresh from your local fishmarket if you prefer.

Separating head and entrails from body

Removing backbone from squid

Removing skin from squid hood

1kg squid
2 cloves garlic, crushed
1/3 cup balsamic vinegar (80ml)
1/3 cup olive oil (80ml)
1/2 long loaf pide
1 medium red onion (170g), chopped finely
100g baby rocket leaves
1/2 cup niçoise olives (90g), seeded
8 large fresh basil leaves, torn

1 Gently pull head and entrails away from squid body. Remove and discard the clear backbone (the quill) and the flaps and skin from hood, dipping your fingers in salt to help keep a grip on the slippery squid. Cut squid hood into 2cm rings.

2 Combine rings in large bowl with garlic, half of the vinegar and half of the oil, cover; refrigerate 3 hours or overnight.

3 Drain rings; discard marinade. Char-grill (or barbecue or pan-fry) rings, in batches, until browned all over and just cooked through, brushing with reserved marinade during cooking.

4 Meanwhile, halve bread lengthways; cut each piece into halves, toast or grill both sides.

5 Combine calamari rings in large bowl with remaining ingredients; gently toss to combine. Serve calamari salad with toasted bread.

SERVES 4

per serve 22.9g fat; 1949kJ

tips

- Marinating the octopus or calamari tenderises it and lends it a fuller flavour, so marinating it overnight greatly enhances the flavour.
- Char-grilling octopus or calamari on your barbecue gives great results, but browning it on your stovetop – the way it's prepared in restaurants – is equally good.
- Baby spinach or cos lettuce leaves, kalamata or big cracked green olives, pocket or large pieces of pitta bread can be mixed and matched with the cooked calamari with equal success, although we recommend you stick with the balsamic vinegar for its special rich and tangy flavour. Use extra virgin olive oil if you can.

cajun blackened fish with corn and tomato salsa

PREPARATION TIME 10 MINUTES • COOKING TIME 10 MINUTES

Cajun cooking, originating in Louisiana, is a blend of French, African and indigenous American styles used to prepare the seafood and vegetables native to that sultry, swampy region of the United States.

Coating fish in spice mixture

Removing husk and silk from corn

Cutting corn kernels from cob

Seeding tomatoes

3 teaspoons onion salt
3 teaspoons hot paprika
3 teaspoons freshly ground black pepper
3 teaspoons ground oregano
1/2 teaspoon chilli powder
12 small boneless white fish fillets (1kg)
2 tablespoons olive oil

CORN AND TOMATO SALSA
2 corn cobs (800g)
1 small red onion (100g), chopped finely
5 medium egg tomatoes (375g), seeded, chopped finely
1 tablespoon finely chopped fresh coriander leaves
2 tablespoons fresh lime juice
1 tablespoon olive oil

1 Combine salt, paprika, pepper, oregano and chilli powder on tray or in medium bowl; working with one piece at a time, coat fish fillets, both sides, in spice mixture.

2 Heat 1 tablespoon of the oil in a large heavy-base frying pan; cook fish, in batches, about 2 minutes each side or until cooked as desired and coating has "blackened". Repeat with remaining oil and fish.
Serve blackened fish with salsa.

corn and tomato salsa Remove and discard husk and silk from corn; cut kernels from cobs. Boil, steam or microwave corn kernels until just tender. When corn has cooled, combine with remaining ingredients in medium serving bowl.

SERVES 4

per serve 19.1g fat; 2012kJ

tips

- We've blended our own Cajun spice mix, but you can buy it ready-made (usually called Cajun Seasoning) in the spice section of your supermarket.
- Select a fairly dry fish (silver warehou, snapper, trevally, dhufish, etc) and it will be less likely to lose the spice coating when it comes into contact with heat.
- It is easiest to cut the kernels off a corn cob before the corn has been cooked. Using a sharp knife, slice between the kernels and cob in one smooth motion down the length of the cob. Continue, turning the cob, until all kernels have been removed.

Deveining shelled prawns

Slicing cucumber on the diagonal

Trimming the watercress

Thinly slicing mint leaves

prawn and mint salad

PREPARATION TIME 30 MINUTES

This salad makes a good main course for a light meal.

40 medium cooked prawns (1kg)
1 Lebanese cucumber (130g)
3 cups snow pea tendrils (60g)
3 cups watercress (60g)
2 cups bean sprouts (160g)
1 tablespoon fish sauce
1/4 cup fresh lime juice (60ml)
1/2 cup coconut milk (125ml)
2 tablespoons sugar
1 clove garlic, crushed
2 teaspoons grated fresh ginger
1 small red Thai chilli, sliced finely
1/2 cup thinly sliced fresh mint leaves

1 Shell and devein prawns, leaving tails intact. Halve cucumber lengthways, slice thinly on the diagonal.

2 Trim then wash snow pea tendrils, watercress and sprouts in cold water; dry completely (use a salad spinner if you have one).

3 Whisk sauce, juice, milk, sugar, garlic, ginger and chilli in large bowl until well mixed; add prawns, cucumber and remaining ingredients, toss salad gently to combine.

SERVES 4

per serve 8.7g fat; 1087kJ

serving suggestion You need little else with this salad but a loaf of good fresh bread.

tips

- If you like, buy uncooked prawns and marinate them overnight in a little fresh lime juice, then barbecue and serve on top of the other salad ingredients.
- Substitute the snow pea tendrils with snow pea sprouts if you like, and use any of the different cresses available at your greengrocers instead of the watercress.
- The coconut milk can be substituted with 1/4 cup of good-quality nut oil (macadamia, walnut, etc) if you don't want the taste of coconut in this salad. If you use a nut oil, try tossing in 250g of cooked and cooled thin rice noodles to make the salad a more filling meal.

tips

- We used fresh flathead fillets here, but you can use any firm white fish – try blue-eye, bream, sea perch, swordfish, tuna or whiting.
- Pontiac potatoes are one of the best potatoes for making chips because, once cut into chips or wedges, they crisp beautifully on the outside while maintaining a light and fluffy interior. Rather than making chips, you can cut each potato into 8 wedges before placing on oven trays and baking.
- Make a mock tartare sauce by stirring the gherkins, capers and chives into a cup of plain yogurt – it won't have the zing of the real thing but you'll certainly reduce the fat count.

oven-baked fish 'n' chips with tartare sauce

PREPARATION TIME 35 MINUTES • COOKING TIME 50 MINUTES

This is a more contemporary, lower-fat version of fish 'n' chips – no less delicious but certainly fewer kilojoules!

1kg pontiac potatoes
cooking-oil spray
12 firm white fish fillets (750g)
1/4 cup plain flour (35g)
3 egg whites, beaten lightly
1 tablespoon low-fat milk
2 1/4 cups stale breadcrumbs (155g)
3/4 cup cornflake crumbs (75g)

TARTARE SAUCE
2 egg yolks
1 tablespoon lemon juice
1/2 teaspoon salt
1/2 teaspoon mustard powder
1 cup vegetable oil (250ml)
2 tablespoons milk, approximately
2 tablespoons chopped gherkins
2 tablespoons drained capers, chopped
2 tablespoons chopped fresh chives

1 Preheat oven to moderately hot.

2 Cut peeled potatoes into 1.5cm slices; cut slices into 1cm chips. Place potato chips, in single layer, on oven tray; coat lightly with cooking-oil spray. Bake, uncovered, in moderately hot oven about 35 minutes or until brown.

3 Meanwhile, working with 1 fillet at a time, toss fish in flour, shake off excess; dip fish into combined egg white and milk, then combined crumbs. Place on oiled oven tray; repeat with remainder of fish. Bake fish, uncovered, in moderately hot oven for the final 20 minutes of chip baking time. Serve fish 'n' chips with tartare sauce.

tartare sauce Blend or process egg yolks, juice, salt and mustard until smooth. With motor operating, add oil gradually, in thin stream; process until sauce thickens. Place sauce in serving bowl; whisk in only enough milk to give desired consistency then stir in remaining ingredients.

SERVES 4

per serve fish 6.2g fat; 1612kJ chips 1.5g fat; 626kJ
tartare sauce (per 2-tablespoon serve) 26.3g fat; 1007kJ

Cutting potatoes into chips

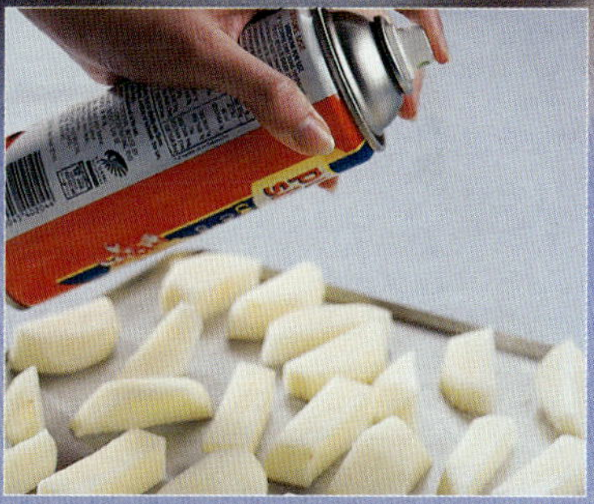

Spraying chips with oil

Coating fish in combined crumbs

tips

- Niçoise olives are small, brownish-black, pointy-ended olives grown in Provence, the French region on the Mediterranean near Monaco. Substitute them with kalamata olives if you wish.
- If you are in a hurry and haven't got fresh fish, drain a 425g can of tuna in oil, then toss the flaked fish into the salad along with the onion, tomato, beans and so forth.

Thinly slicing onion wedges

Removing seeds from tomatoes

Shredding basil

salade niçoise

PREPARATION TIME 35 MINUTES • COOKING TIME 5 MINUTES

There are many versions of this popular salad but an authentic salade niçoise, originating from the city of Nice on the French Mediterranean, always includes the sun-kissed best of the region's produce: tomatoes, capers, olives and garlic. Other regular inclusions are anchovies, tuna, hard-boiled egg, artichoke hearts, radishes, diced cooked potato, and green or red capsicum.

1 medium red onion (170g)
4 medium egg tomatoes (300g)
3 trimmed celery sticks (225g)
3 hard-boiled eggs
200g green beans
12 whole canned anchovy fillets, drained, halved lengthways
2 x 450g fresh tuna steaks
100g niçoise olives, seeded
2 tablespoons baby capers
2 tablespoons finely shredded fresh basil leaves

LEMON GARLIC DRESSING
1/2 cup extra virgin olive oil (125ml)
1/4 cup lemon juice (60ml)
1 clove garlic, crushed
1 teaspoon sugar

1 Quarter onion lengthways; slice thinly. Cut tomatoes into wedges; remove seeds. Slice celery thinly. Cut hard-boiled eggs into quarters.

2 Top and tail beans; boil, steam or microwave until just tender; drain.

3 Char-grill, barbecue or pan-fry tuna, both sides, until cooked as desired; cut into 3cm pieces.

4 Layer onion, tomato, beans, celery, egg, anchovies and tuna on large serving platter. Sprinkle with olives, capers and basil; drizzle with dressing.

lemon garlic dressing Combine ingredients in screw-top jar; shake well.

SERVES 4

per serve 61.3g fat; 751kJ

vegetables

for your information...

Salting and standing a chopped eggplant is called "disgorging" – the eggplant's bitter juices are drawn out by the salt and washed away when you rinse off the salt. This is an important step in the preparation of any recipe that features eggplant as a main ingredient.

Salad greens should be removed from their stems, if desired, rinsed well in a few changes of cold water, then dried completely. A salad spinner is a good investment if you eat a lot of salads – the greens can be washed, thoroughly dried and crisped in the refrigerator using this one handy kitchen appliance.

Of the many potato varieties available, some are well suited to particular cooking methods. For mashed potato, try pink fir apple, sebago, bintje, desiree, king edward or nicola; for salads, try waxy potatoes like coliban, pink-eye or new; and for roasting and wedges, give pontiac, kipfler, sebago, desiree or king edward a try.

Almost every vegetable can be stir-fried successfully and, if you use a well-seasoned wok, you need to add very little oil. Make sure vegetables are as dry as possible before stir-frying them, to prevent their becoming soggy.

stir-fried asian greens

PREPARATION TIME 10 MINUTES • COOKING TIME 10 MINUTES

For good reason, stir-frying has been the main way of cooking vegetables in Asia for thousands of years – preparation and cooking times are minimal but retention of nutrients and development of flavours are maximised.

Discarding tough stems from choy sum

Slicing ends of stems from tat soi

Slicing baby bok choy in half lengthways

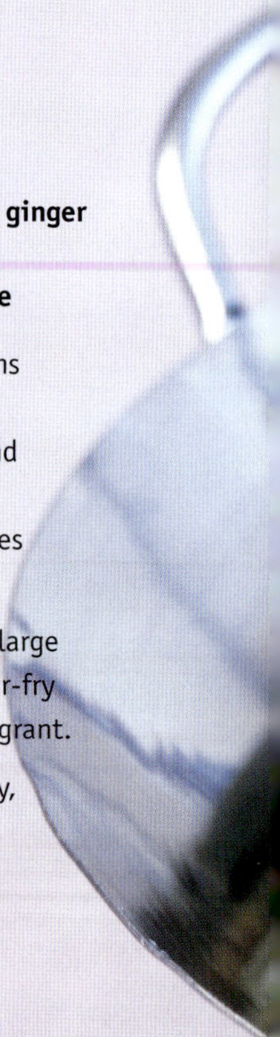

1kg baby bok choy
500g choy sum
300g tat soi
1 tablespoon peanut oil
2 cloves garlic, crushed
2 teaspoons grated fresh ginger
1 tablespoon soy sauce
1 tablespoon oyster sauce

1. Slice away bottom of stems and any unsightly leaves on bok choy, choy sum and tat soi; halve bok choy lengthways, separate leaves of vegetables.
2. Add oil to heated wok or large heavy-base frying pan; stir-fry garlic and ginger until fragrant.
3. Add greens to wok; stir-fry, tossing, until just wilted.
4. Stir in sauces; toss gently until heated through.

SERVES 4

per serve 5.3g fat; 392kJ

tips

- The sauces used help prevent vegetables sticking to the pan, as well as imparting flavours. If you prefer, there are a myriad bottled sauces you can substitute to produce incredibly diverse results.
- Baby bok choy is sometimes called Shanghai bok choy, Chinese chard or white cabbage, or baby pak choi, and has a mildly acrid, appealing taste.
- Choy sum is easy to identify, with its long stems and yellow flowers (hence its other common name, flowering cabbage). It is eaten stems and all.
- Tat soi (also known as rosette bok choy) has a mild cabbagey, slightly bitter taste. Its flower-like leaves should be eaten soon after harvest because it gets unpleasantly strong after a few days.

Cooling the hard-boiled eggs

Finely chopping green onions

Boiling chopped potatoes

Cooking bacon in a dry frying pan

potato salad

PREPARATION TIME 20 MINUTES (plus cooling time)
COOKING TIME 15 MINUTES

We used the large, white, washed coliban variety of potato in this recipe; other good waxy potatoes for salad are new and pink-eye.

3 large potatoes (900g), chopped coarsely
2 bacon rashers, chopped
3 hard-boiled eggs, quartered
1 trimmed celery stick (75g), chopped finely
3 green onions, chopped finely
2 dill pickles, chopped finely
$1/4$ cup mayonnaise (60ml)
$1/4$ cup sour cream (60ml)
2 tablespoons French dressing
1 teaspoon seeded mustard

1 Boil, steam or microwave potato until just tender; drain. Rinse potato under cold water to halt further cooking; drain.

2 Meanwhile, cook bacon in medium dry frying pan until crisp; drain on absorbent paper.

3 Combine potato, bacon, egg, celery, onion and pickle in large bowl; mix gently. Stir in combined mayonnaise, cream, dressing and mustard; toss gently to combine.

SERVES 4

per serve 20g fat; 1462kJ

tips

- A good rule when preparing an old-fashioned potato salad is to use 1 egg for every large potato. Cool the hard-boiled eggs with their shells cracked in a large bowl of cold water; this makes them easier to shell and helps prevent discolouration.
- Peeling and chopping the potatoes into manageable, similar-size pieces before cooking helps control their degree of tenderness.
- If you prefer to omit the bacon, use 4 trimmed celery sticks.
- Use light sour cream instead of the mayonnaise and regular sour cream if you are counting kilojoules.
- Finely chopped fresh French tarragon provides a complementary flavour to this dressing.

roasted vegetables

traditional roast potatoes

PREPARATION TIME 15 MINUTES
(plus cooling time)
COOKING TIME 55 MINUTES

Several potato varieties are well suited to roasting – sebago, pontiac, desiree, king edward and kipfler. We used sebago, sold in most supermarkets simply called "brushed" potatoes.

1kg potatoes, peeled, halved
2 tablespoons olive oil

1 Boil, steam or microwave potato until just tender, drain.
2 Preheat oven to hot.
3 When potato is cool enough to handle, gently scratch potato surface with a fork.
4 Place potato, cut-side down, on large oiled oven tray; brush potato all over with oil. Roast, uncovered, in hot oven about 50 minutes or until potato is browned and crisp.

SERVES 4

per serve 9.7g fat; 1004kJ

Placing potatoes in microwave-safe bowl

Scratching surface of potatoes with a fork

roasted rosemary potatoes

PREPARATION TIME 10 MINUTES
COOKING TIME 50 MINUTES

The red-skinned pontiac is one of the oldest cultivated varieties of potato and is certainly one of the best for roasting.

1 bunch fresh rosemary
cooking-oil spray
1kg pontiac potatoes, unpeeled, quartered
2 tablespoons olive oil
3 cloves garlic, crushed

1 Preheat oven to hot.
2 Place rosemary in single layer to cover oven tray, spray with oil.
3 Combine remaining ingredients in large bowl, stirring to coat potato in oil.
4 Place potato on rosemary stems; roast, uncovered, in hot oven about 50 minutes or until potato is browned and tender, turning once midway through cooking time.

SERVES 4

per serve 10.1g fat; 1029kJ

Placing potatoes on a bed of rosemary

tips You can "roll" the potatoes in a plastic bag containing the olive oil and garlic until they are coated, to avoid dirtying a bowl. Squeeze any remaining garlic and oil onto the potatoes once they've been placed on the rosemary.

- Rosemary can be frozen in airtight plastic bags; there is no need to thaw it for this recipe.

Trimming roots from onions and shallots

Adding eggplant and tomatoes to dish

roasted baby vegetables

PREPARATION TIME 15 MINUTES • COOKING TIME 40 MINUTES

Shallots (occasionally known as eschalots) are very mild small brown onions. Baby onions, also small and brown, are sometimes called pickling onions. Both varieties are excellent when slow-roasted, both with other small vegetables and on their own.

500g baby onions
250g shallots
2 tablespoons olive oil
1kg tiny new potatoes, unpeeled
6 baby eggplants (360g), halved lengthways
250g cherry tomatoes

1 Trim off roots and remove cores of onions and shallots, discard roots and cores.

2 Preheat oven to hot.

3 Heat oil in large flameproof baking dish; cook onions, shallots and potatoes, stirring, until vegetables are browned all over.

4 Roast vegetables, uncovered, in hot oven about 20 minutes, or until potatoes are almost tender. Add eggplant and tomatoes to baking dish; roast, uncovered, another 10 minutes or until eggplant is browned and tender.

SERVES 4

per serve 10.2g fat; 1263kJ

tips Tiny new potatoes are also known as chats; they're not a variety but an early harvest, having a thin pale skin that is easily rubbed off. New potatoes are good steamed as well as roasted, and can be eaten hot or cold in salads.

- There are many different baby vegetables suitable for roasting to be found at the greengrocer's. Look for baby beetroot, turnips, carrots and so forth – they're beautifully sweet and flavoursome.

ratatouille

PREPARATION TIME 20 MINUTES (plus standing time)
COOKING TIME 20 MINUTES

Traditionally cooked on top of the stove (as in our main recipe), ratatouille can also be cooked in the oven (see below right). We give you both options here, but the consistency of the dish when cooked in the oven will be more stewy.

2 medium zucchini (240g)
1 large eggplant (500g)
coarse cooking salt
1 medium red capsicum (200g)
1 medium yellow capsicum (200g)
1 medium green capsicum (200g)
1/4 cup olive oil (60ml)
1 medium brown onion (150g), chopped coarsely
2 cloves garlic, crushed
6 large egg tomatoes (540g), peeled, quartered
1/4 cup firmly packed torn fresh basil leaves

tips

- This Provençale vegetable dish is a great Mediterranean classic, and is delicious eaten hot or cooled. When serving at room temperature, stir a few tablespoons of extra virgin olive oil into the dish to achieve a special velvety smoothness.
- The eggplant and zucchini are weighted to extract as much of their natural juices as possible: if left, this liquid causes the vegetables to soften unattractively when cooked. This process is called disgorging, and also helps keep eggplant and zucchini from absorbing too much oil when cooked.
- Put more, rather than less, salt on the vegetables; if you rinse the drained zucchini and eggplant well in several changes of cold water, the ratatouille won't be oversalted.

1 Cut zucchini and eggplant into 3cm pieces; place vegetables in sieve or colander, sprinkle with salt. Place a plate on top of vegetables, weigh down with a heavy can; stand 30 minutes.

2 Meanwhile, halve capsicums; discard seeds and membranes. Cut capsicums into 3cm-square pieces.

3 Rinse zucchini and eggplant under cold water; pat dry with absorbent paper.

4 Heat 1 tablespoon of the oil in large heavy-base frying pan; cook onion and garlic, stirring, until onion is soft; remove from pan.

5 Heat half of the remaining oil in same pan; cook zucchini and eggplant, in batches, until just tender. Add remaining oil to same pan; cook capsicums, in batches, until just tender.

6 Place onion mixture and tomato in same pan, bring to boil; simmer, uncovered, about 15 minutes or until sauce thickens slightly. Add zucchini, eggplant, capsicums and basil; heat briefly, occasionally stirring gently, until ratatouille is hot.

SERVES 4

per serve 15.5g fat; 904kJ

Salting the zucchini and eggplant

Weighting the zucchini and eggplant

Removing seeds from capsicums

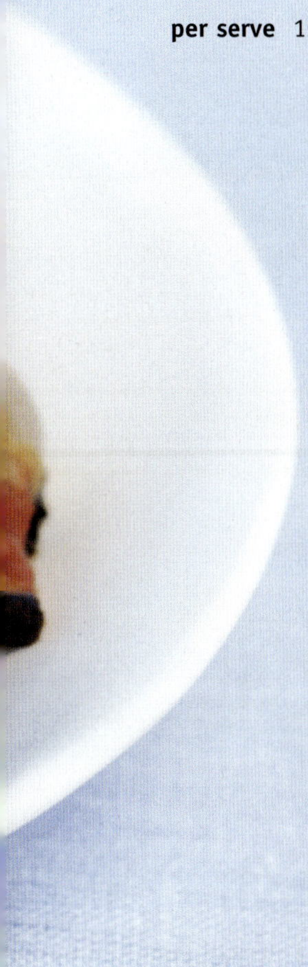

oven-baked ratatouille

PREPARATION TIME 20 MINUTES
(plus standing time)
COOKING TIME 45 MINUTES

Proceed with main recipe through steps 1 to 3; preheat oven to very hot. Combine zucchini, eggplant and capsicums in large shallow baking dish with onion and tomato; drizzle with combined oil and garlic. Bake ratatouille, uncovered, in very hot oven about 40 minutes or until vegetables are tender and starting to brown on the edges; stir in basil.

mixed green salad

PREPARATION TIME 15 MINUTES

We are spoilt for choice today – there are at least a dozen different leafy greens available at virtually every greengrocer's. Mix and match the varieties to decide on a combination that suits you best. And don't overlook the humble iceberg – for adaptability and crunch, it's hard to beat.

1/2 medium butter lettuce
1/2 medium iceberg lettuce
1 baby cos lettuce
1 medium green capsicum (200g)
2 Lebanese cucumbers (260g)
1 small white onion (80g)

1 Core and remove thick white stems from lettuces; wash in cold water, dry leaves thoroughly.

2 Cut capsicum crossways into thin rings; discard seeds and membrane. Slice unpeeled cucumbers on the diagonal; slice onion thinly, separate rings.

3 Tear lettuce leaves into bite-size pieces; combine in large bowl with capsicum, cucumber and onion. Drizzle with salad dressing of your choice, if desired.

SERVES 4

per serve 0.4g fat; 144kJ (excluding dressing)

Removing core from iceberg lettuce

Drying lettuce with a salad spinner

Preparing cucumber, capsicum and onion

french dressing

Blend 1/4 cup white vinegar (60ml), 3/4 cup olive oil (180ml), 1/2 teaspoon sugar and 1 teaspoon Dijon mustard in small bowl or jug until well combined.

MAKES ABOUT 1 CUP (250ml)

per 60ml serve 43g fat; 1605kJ

italian dressing

Make French dressing (above), then add 2 crushed cloves of garlic, 1 tablespoon each of finely chopped fresh flat-leaf parsley and finely chopped fresh basil, and about 1/4 cup of finely chopped fresh red capsicum.

MAKES ABOUT 1 CUP (250ml)

per 60ml serve 43g fat; 1626kJ

tips

- Experiment with different combinations of oils and vinegars. You'll soon see that one particular vinegar or oil will harmonise with an individual green better than others; for instance, rocket and balsamic vinegar seem to have been invented to be served together.
- It's best not to wash more lettuce than you'll need for one meal because, even under the best conditions, the greens can "rust" overnight; keep the remainder of your unwashed lettuce wrapped tightly in plastic wrap, in the crisper of your refrigerator.

thai red curry vegetables

PREPARATION TIME 20 MINUTES • COOKING TIME 20 MINUTES

Serve steamed jasmine rice with this rich and creamy vegetable curry. Try adding 6 bruised cardamom pods to the rice before cooking to give it a sweet perfume.

1 tablespoon peanut oil
1 large leek (500g), sliced thinly
2 cloves garlic, crushed
1 large red Thai chilli, seeded, chopped finely
1/3 cup Thai red curry paste (90g)
2 medium carrots (240g), chopped coarsely
3 sticks trimmed celery (225g), sliced thinly
400g can tomatoes
1 2/3 cups coconut cream (400ml)
1 cup vegetable stock (250ml)
300g cauliflower, cut into small florets
1 medium kumara (400g), cut into 3cm pieces
175g snake beans, chopped into 4cm lengths
4 kaffir lime leaves
1/4 cup coarsely chopped fresh coriander leaves

1 Heat the oil in large saucepan; cook leek, garlic and chilli, stirring until leek is just soft.

2 Add paste to pan; cook, stirring, until mixture is fragrant. Add carrot and celery; cook, stirring, 5 minutes. Add undrained crushed tomatoes, coconut cream and stock, bring to boil; simmer, uncovered, 10 minutes.

3 Add cauliflower, kumara, beans and lime leaves; simmer, uncovered, another 15 minutes or until kumara is just tender. Stir through coriander; simmer, uncovered, about 5 minutes or until curry sauce thickens.

SERVES 4

per serve 30.6g fat; 1863kJ

tips

- You can use other commercially prepared Thai curry pastes instead of the red in this recipe if you wish: try the same amount of green, yellow or massaman varieties.
- Vary the vegetable selection – bean sprouts, bamboo shoots, tiny Thai eggplant, even peas, can be used instead of (or with) the vegetables we've used here.
- Kaffir lime leaves can be frozen successfully; freeze in an airtight plastic bag and take what you need for each recipe from its contents.

Stirring curry paste into leek mixture

Adding vegetables to curry in batches

fruit

for your information...

Where a recipe calls for citrus rind, feel free to experiment with different varieties: orange, lemon, lime or mandarin, or any combination thereof. Remember, though, to avoid using the bitter white pith when grating citrus rind.

Two apple varieties that stand up well to baking are granny smith and golden delicious.

Puddings and cakes containing a lot of fruit or sugar can stick to the pan they're cooked in: lining the base of the pan with baking paper helps prevent this.

impossible pie

PREPARATION TIME 15 MINUTES • COOKING TIME 45 MINUTES

This dessert is "easy-as-pie" to make – all the ingredients are mixed in a single bowl.

Whisking eggs together

Whisking flour into the egg mixture

Grating lemon finely

Pouring pie mixture into prepared pan

4 eggs
1/2 cup plain flour (75g)
1 cup caster sugar (220g)
1 cup desiccated coconut (90g)
125g butter, melted
300ml thickened cream
3/4 cup milk (180ml)
1 tablespoon finely grated lemon rind
1/4 cup lemon juice (60ml)

1. Preheat oven to moderate. Grease straight-sided deep 19cm-square cake pan.
2. Whisk eggs in large bowl; gradually whisk in flour then remaining ingredients until mixture is well combined. Pour mixture into prepared pan.
3. Bake, uncovered, in moderate oven about 45 minutes or until pie is browned and set. If serving warm, stand pie in pan for 20 minutes before cutting; if serving cold, cool in the pan to room temperature or refrigerate, covered, until serving time. Cut pie into 6 pieces; remove from pan using eggslice. Serve dusted with sifted icing sugar and extra citrus rind, if desired, accompanied by the fruit of your choice.

SERVES 6

per serve 49.8g fat; 2813kJ

tips

- Impossible pie will keep, covered, under refrigeration for up to 3 days.
- This dessert is called "impossible" because, while a runny mixture is poured into the cake pan, it is a three-layered "pie" that emerges from the oven. The bottom layer is pastry-like because the flour and butter sink to the bottom; the centre layer is like a custard filling; and the top is slightly browned and crusty because the coconut, the lightest ingredient, floats to the top during baking.

apple cake

PREPARATION TIME 25 MINUTES • COOKING TIME 1 HOUR

185g butter, chopped
2 teaspoons finely grated orange rind
2/3 cup caster sugar (150g)
3 eggs
1 cup self-raising flour (150g)
1/2 cup plain flour (75g)
1/3 cup milk (80ml)
2 medium apples (300g)
1/3 cup marmalade (90g), warmed, strained

1 Grease deep 22cm-round cake pan; line base with baking paper. Preheat oven to moderate.

2 Beat butter, rind and sugar in medium bowl with electric mixer until light and fluffy. Beat in eggs, 1 at a time, until combined.

3 Sift about half the flours over butter mixture, add about half the milk; stir with a wooden spoon only until combined. Stir in remaining sifted flours and milk until mixture is smooth. Spread cake mixture evenly into prepared pan.

4 Peel, quarter and core apples. Make several closely placed cuts in the rounded side of each apple quarter, slicing about three-quarters of the way through each piece. Place quarters, rounded-side up, around outer edge of the cake. Bake in moderate oven about 1 hour or until cooked when tested. Stand cake 5 minutes before turning onto wire rack. Remove paper, turn cake right way up onto another rack. Brush warm marmalade over top of hot cake; cool before cutting.

SERVES 8

per serve 21.6g fat; 1721kJ

serving suggestions This cake is good served as a warm dessert with cream, custard or ice-cream.

tips

- Warm marmalade in a bowl or jug in the microwave oven for about 30 seconds, then push through strainer to remove large pieces of rind.
- Always beat flavourings such as essences and rinds with the butter in cakes, biscuits, etc – the flavours will be more intense in the finished product.
- Caster sugar gives a finer-textured cake, but you can substitute regular table sugar.
- Butter is best, but you can use a cooking margarine if you prefer.
- We used granny smith apples, but golden delicious are a good substitute; both varieties stand up well when baked.

Lining cake pan with baking paper

Beating butter, rind and sugar until fluffy

Sifting flours over the butter mixture

Folding short ends of pastry

Slicing the unpeeled nashi into rounds

Placing cooked nashi on pastry pieces

Brushing nashi with melted butter mixture

Boiling reserved syrup to a thick glaze

nashi galette

PREPARATION TIME 15 MINUTES • COOKING TIME 1 HOUR 15 MINUTES

Galette is a French term for a flat tart that can be round or rectangular, sweet or savoury, and topped with myriad fillings. In our particular variation of this flaky-pastry dessert, you can use either pear or apple, or a combination of both, rather than the nashi.

2 sheets ready-rolled puff pastry
3 medium nashi (900g)
1/2 teaspoon finely grated lime rind
1/4 cup lime juice (60ml)
1/4 cup water (60ml)
1/2 cup caster sugar (110g)
2 tablespoons green ginger wine
30g butter, melted
1 tablespoon brown sugar

1 Cut pastry sheets in half; place two halves on each of two lightly greased oven trays. Fold long sides of each pastry piece in about 2cm; press folded sections lightly then turn short ends in, making three small folds in each.

2 Cut whole unpeeled nashi into 1cm slices. Discard small end slices; you need 16 similar-size nashi rounds for this recipe. Preheat oven to hot.

3 Combine rind, juice, the water, caster sugar and wine in large heavy-base frying pan; stir over high heat without boiling until sugar is dissolved. Bring to a boil, add nashi to syrup, in batches if necessary; cook over low heat about 10 minutes or until just tender. Remove nashi from syrup with a slotted spoon, reserving as much syrup in pan as possible.

4 Place nashi slices on pastry pieces; brush with combined melted butter and brown sugar. Bake in hot oven, uncovered, about 20 minutes or until browned.

5 Meanwhile, boil reserved syrup about 10 minutes or until reduced to a thick glaze; brush hot galettes with glaze.

SERVES 4

per serve 25.3g fat; 2453kJ

tips

- All puff-pastry desserts are best if eaten soon after they've been baked; however, they can be kept, covered, under refrigeration, up to three days.
- As puff pastry contains a great deal of fat, it's not always necessary to grease the baking dish or oven tray. In this recipe, though, the sugar can melt onto the baking surface and cause the galettes to stick, so we suggest greasing the trays lightly in the spots where the galettes will sit.
- Green ginger wine is rich with the taste of fresh ginger; use white dry vermouth if you prefer, or even a tablespoon of syrup from a jar of preserved ginger.
- The size of your frying pan will determine whether you need to cook the nashi in batches. The fruit slices should not overlap in the syrup or they won't cook evenly.

tips

- We recommend you use an aluminium cake pan for this recipe.
- Puddings and cakes containing a lot of fruit and sugar can stick to the pan they're cooked in; lining the base of the pan with baking paper helps prevent this.
- It's not necessary to sift the flour or pack it tightly into the measuring cup; just shake it in then tap the cup once or twice on the bench to settle the flour.
- The pudding keeps up to a week if stored in an airtight container; in a humid climate, keep it under refrigeration. The sauce will keep, in a clean glass jar with a tight-fitting lid, for about 2 months under refrigeration. The chilled sauce will separate into distinct layers but will come together again once reheated.

sticky date pudding with caramel sauce

PREPARATION TIME 15 MINUTES (plus standing time) • COOKING TIME 55 MINUTES

1½ cups seeded dried dates (250g)
1¼ cups boiling water (310ml)
1 teaspoon bicarbonate of soda
cooking-oil spray
¾ cup firmly packed brown sugar (150g)
60g butter
2 eggs
1 cup self-raising flour (150g)

CARAMEL SAUCE
1 cup firmly packed brown sugar (200g)
100g butter, chopped
300ml cream

1 Adjust oven shelves so a deep 20cm-round cake pan fits on the top shelf, as close to the centre of oven as possible. Preheat oven to moderate.

2 Put dates, the water and soda into bowl of food processor, place lid on processor; let mixture stand 5 minutes.

3 Grease base and side of the cake pan evenly with cooking-oil spray; line base of pan with a round of baking paper.

4 Add brown sugar and chopped butter to date mixture; process, by pulsing, about 5 seconds or until dates are roughly chopped.

5 Add eggs, then flour; process, by pulsing, for 5 to 10 seconds, until all ingredients are combined. Scrape any unmixed flour back into the mixture with a rubber spatula; pulse again to combine ingredients.

6 Pour pudding mixture into prepared pan. Cook, uncovered, in moderate oven 55 minutes. To test if pudding is cooked, gently press the top with two fingers; it should feel firm and appear slightly shrunken from side of pan. Push a skewer through the centre of the pudding to bottom of pan; the skewer should be greasy when withdrawn but free of uncooked mixture. If pudding needs additional cooking, return it to oven for 5 minutes. Once cooked and removed from oven, stand 5 minutes in pan.

7 Put a wire rack on top of pan and, holding both rack and pan, turn pudding upside down. Remove pan then baking paper. Put a second wire rack on pudding; holding racks together firmly but not digging into pudding, turn so pudding is top-side up. Serve pudding hot, cut into wedges, with warm caramel sauce.

caramel sauce Place sugar and butter in medium saucepan over high heat; using wooden spoon, stir in the cream. Once butter melts, bring sauce to a boil (to prevent it boiling over, either lower the heat or remove pan from heat for a moment). Stir sauce constantly until completely smooth; serve while hot.

SERVES 8

per serve 31.7g fat; 2523kJ

serving suggestions Vanilla ice-cream, whipped or thick cream, and any kind of berries are all great accompaniments. This pudding can also be served as a cake.

Adding soda to the dates and water

Adding brown sugar and butter to processor

Pouring pudding mixture into prepared pan

sugar syrup variations

Complete step 1 of the main recipe to create 1 portion of basic sugar syrup.

oranges in sugar syrup

Remove skin and white pith from 4 large oranges (1.2kg); slice thickly. Add 1 tablespoon Grand Marnier and orange slices to 1 portion basic sugar syrup. Stir until coated with syrup; serve with whipped cream.

fruit compote

Add 130g each of dried pears, apricots and peaches, 100g of fresh or dried dates, prunes or raisins, and 80g of dried apple to 1 portion basic sugar syrup. Stir over low heat until fruit softens slightly. Serve warm over porridge, creamed rice, ice-cream or yogurt.

strawberries in sugar syrup

Simmer 1 portion basic sugar syrup with 2 cinnamon sticks, strips of rind from 1 lime, and 2 teaspoons peppermint essence or crème de menthe; spoon over fresh strawberries.

berry marshmallow sorbet

Stir 1 tablespoon orange-blossom water into 1 portion basic sugar syrup. Blend or process 300g fresh or thawed frozen blueberries, raspberries or strawberries, or a combination of them, until smooth. With motor operating, gradually add syrup. Strain mixture into large bowl, discard seeds. Beat 3 egg whites in small bowl with electric mixer until soft peaks form; fold whites through berry mixture, in two batches, until well combined. Pour sorbet mixture into 7cm x 25cm bar pan, cover with foil; freeze until almost set. Remove from freezer; place in large bowl, whisk to break up ice crystals. Re-freeze in same bar pan, covered with foil, overnight or until set.

poached pears in sugar syrup

PREPARATION TIME 2 MINUTES
COOKING TIME 15 MINUTES

$2\frac{1}{2}$ cups sugar (550g)
$2\frac{1}{2}$ cups water (625ml)
1 vanilla pod, halved lengthways
7 star anise
8 fresh dates, halved
6 corella pears (1kg), peeled

1. Combine sugar and water in medium saucepan, stir over high heat, without boiling, until sugar is dissolved. Bring to boil; simmer without stirring, uncovered, about 15 minutes or until thickened slightly.
2. Add vanilla pod, star anise and dates to syrup.
3. Add the pears, fitting them snugly in pan so they remain upright when being poached. Simmer, covered, about 20 minutes or until tender. Serve pears with syrup.

SERVES 6

per serve 0.2g fat; 1192kJ

Brushing undissolved sugar from side of pan

Peeling pears before poaching

Fitting pears tightly into pan with syrup

tips

- We used water for the basic syrup, however lemon, orange or lime juice can be substituted.
- Other spices and flavourings can be added to the basic sugar syrup after it has thickened (end of step 1) – try any one of these: 2 cinnamon sticks; 1 vanilla bean and 5 cloves; 5 bruised cardamom pods; 1/2 teaspoon of an essence such as peppermint, mint, coffee, lemon or orange; 1 tablespoon of grated rind from an orange, lime or lemon; 2 tablespoons of a liqueur such as Cointreau, Midori, crème de cassis, marsala, crème de menthe or crème de cacao.

chocolate

for your information...

Care must be taken when melting chocolate that it does not come into contact with water. If it does, it will "seize", that is, become lumpy and lose its sheen. If this occurs, you'll have to start over with a new piece of chocolate. For this reason, never cover chocolate when melting it: the condensation that forms inside a saucepan lid will drop beads of moisture into the chocolate.

If you melt chocolate over a pan of water or in a double saucepan, be careful that the bottom of the container holding the chocolate does not touch the hot water; the heat of the water will cause the chocolate to burn.

Don't melt chocolate in a plastic bowl because plastic is not a good heat conductor. One of the best ways to melt chocolate is in an uncovered microwave-safe container on HIGH (100%) in 30-second bursts, removing it immediately when melted.

chocolate mousse

PREPARATION TIME 15 MINUTES
COOKING TIME 5 MINUTES (plus cooling time)

Melting chocolate with half the cream

Folding egg whites into chocolate mixture

200g dark chocolate
300ml thickened cream
3 eggs, separated
2 tablespoons caster sugar

1 Break off and reserve a long piece of the chocolate, weighing about 25g, for making decorative chocolate shavings.

2 Chop remaining chocolate coarsely then combine it with half of the cream in large heatproof bowl. Place bowl over saucepan of simmering water; stir until melted. Cool chocolate mixture for 5 minutes then stir in egg yolks, 1 at a time.

3 Beat egg whites in small bowl on highest speed with electric mixer until soft peaks form; add sugar, beat until dissolved. Gently fold whites, in two batches, into chocolate mixture; pour mixture into four 2/3-cup (160ml) serving glasses. Refrigerate several hours or overnight.

4 Whip remaining cream until soft peaks form. Make chocolate shavings by running a vegetable peeler along one edge of the reserved piece of chocolate. Dollop cream and sprinkle chocolate over each mousse.

SERVES 4

per serve 45.8g fat; 2541kJ

tips

- When the egg yolks are stirred into the melted chocolate mixture, work quickly and stir rapidly to avoid the yolks "scrambling" in the still-warm mixture.
- Only beat the egg whites until glossy and barely holding a shape: overbeating makes the whites dry and difficult to fold into the chocolate mixture. When you do fold the whites into the slightly warm chocolate-yolk mixture, do so gently, using a whisk or rubber spatula.

tips

- Brownies can be light and cake-like, fudgy and dense, or moist and chewy – depending on the ratio of chocolate and butter to flour. This recipe produces a brownie that's a happy medium between fudgy and cake-like. Reduce the baking time by 10 minutes if you prefer a more moist brownie.

chocolate fudge brownies

PREPARATION TIME 20 MINUTES • COOKING TIME 45 MINUTES (plus cooling time)

An American classic, brownies are thought to have been "invented" by accident when a New England housewife forgot to add the baking powder to a chocolate cake she was making. Chocolate lovers around the world have enjoyed that result, in one form or another, for more than a century.

¾ cup macadamias (110g)
150g butter
300g dark chocolate, chopped coarsely
1½ cups firmly packed brown sugar (300g)
3 eggs
2 teaspoons vanilla essence
¾ cup plain flour (110g)
¾ cup dark Choc Bits (140g)
½ cup sour cream (125ml)
1 tablespoon cocoa powder

1 Preheat oven to moderate. Line base and sides of 19cm x 29cm rectangular slice pan with baking paper.

2 Toast nuts on oven tray in moderate oven 5 minutes; stir, toast about another 5 minutes or until golden brown all over. Chop nuts coarsely.

3 Melt butter in medium saucepan, add chocolate; stir over low heat, without boiling, until mixture is smooth. Stir in sugar then transfer mixture to large bowl; cool until just warm.

4 Stir in eggs, 1 at a time, then stir in essence, flour, Choc Bits, cream and nuts. Spread mixture into prepared pan; bake, uncovered, in moderate oven about 40 minutes. Cover pan with foil; bake another 20 minutes.

5 Stand brownie slab in pan until it reaches room temperature; turn onto wire rack, remove paper, dust with sifted cocoa. Cut into pieces before serving.

SERVES 12

per serve 33.5g fat; 1897kJ

serving suggestions Brownies are fabulous eaten warm, with a scoop of vanilla ice-cream melting over the top, or cold, accompanied by an equally cold glass of milk. They make a great lunchbox treat.

Stirring brown sugar into chocolate mixture

Adding Choc Bits and nuts to mixture

mud cake with raspberry coulis

PREPARATION TIME 20 MINUTES
COOKING TIME 1 HOUR 50 MINUTES (plus cooling time)

250g butter
1 tablespoon instant coffee powder
$1\frac{1}{2}$ cups hot water (375ml)
2 cups caster sugar (440g)
200g dark chocolate, chopped
$1\frac{1}{2}$ cups self-raising flour (225g)
1 cup plain flour (150g)
$\frac{1}{4}$ cup cocoa powder (25g)
2 eggs
2 teaspoons vanilla essence
150g fresh or frozen raspberries
2 tablespoons cocoa powder, extra

Pouring mixture into prepared pan

Turning cake with wire racks

Pushing raspberries through sieve

1. Preheat oven to slow. Grease deep 22cm-round cake pan; line base and side with baking paper.
2. Melt butter in medium saucepan; dissolve coffee in the hot water then add to pan with sugar and chocolate. Stir chocolate mixture over low heat, without boiling, until smooth. Transfer mixture to large bowl; cool until just warm.
3. Using electric mixer, beat chocolate mixture on low speed; with motor operating, beat in sifted dry ingredients, in three batches. Beat in eggs, 1 at a time, then essence. Pour mixture into prepared pan; bake, uncovered, in slow oven for $1\frac{3}{4}$ hours. Stand cake 15 minutes; turn onto wire rack to cool.
4. Meanwhile, push raspberries through sieve, discard seeds.
5. Dust cake with sifted extra cocoa; serve with coulis, plus cream if desired.

SERVES 8

per serve 35.5g fat; 3288kJ

tips

- This cake is fragile and should not be turned by hand – use racks placed top and bottom. Care must be taken not to squash the cake when manoeuvering the two racks.
- The cake is cooked when: it looks slightly shrunken from the sides of pan; it feels firm when you gently touch the top; you run a metal skewer through the centre of cake to the base of pan and it comes out clean.
- When the cake is cold, it can be stored, in an airtight container, up to 5 days. If the weather is wet or humid, place the container in the refrigerator.

make your own fresh stock...

These recipes can be made up to 4 days ahead and stored, covered, in the refrigerator. Remove any fat from the surface after the cooled stock has been refrigerated overnight. If the stock is to be kept longer, it is best to freeze it in smaller quantities. *All stock recipes make about 2.5 litres (10 cups).* Stock is also available in cans or tetra packs. Stock cubes or powder can be used. As a guide, 1 teaspoon of stock powder or 1 small crumbled stock cube mixed with 1-cup water (250ml) will give a fairly strong stock. Be aware of the salt and fat content of stock cubes and powders, and prepared stocks.

BEEF STOCK

2kg meaty beef bones
2 medium onions (300g), chopped
2 sticks celery, chopped
2 medium carrots (250g), chopped
3 bay leaves
2 teaspoons black peppercorns
5 litres water (20 cups)
3 litres water (20 cups), extra

Combine ingredients in large pan, simmer, uncovered, 2 hours; strain.

VEGETABLE STOCK

2 large carrots (360g), chopped
2 large parsnips (360g), chopped
4 medium onions (600g), chopped
12 sticks celery, chopped
4 bay leaves
2 teaspoons black peppercorns
6 litres water (24 cups)

Combine ingredients in large pan, simmer, uncovered, 1½ hours; strain.

glossary

artichoke hearts centre of the globe artichoke; sold in cans or loose, in brine.

bacon rashers also known as bacon slices.

blue-eye also known as deep sea trevalla or trevally, and blue-eyed cod.

bok choy also called pak choi or Chinese white cabbage.

breadcrumbs, stale day-old bread made into crumbs.

butter 125g is equal to 1 stick butter.

cabbage, chinese also known as Peking cabbage or wong bok.

cajun seasoning packaged blend; can include paprika, basil, onion, fennel, thyme, cayenne and tarragon.

capsicum also known as bell pepper or, simply, pepper.

carambola also called star fruit or five-cornered fruit.

chicken tenderloin strip of meat lying under the breast.

chickpeas also called channa, hummus or garbanzos.

chillies available in many types and sizes. Wear gloves when seeding and chopping fresh chillies: they can burn.

chinese water spinach also known as swamp spinach, long green, ung choy and kang kong.

choy sum also known as flowering bok choy or flowering white cabbage.

coconut

CREAM made from coconut and water.

MILK pure unsweetened coconut milk.

coriander also known as cilantro or Chinese parsley.

cornflour also called corn starch; used as a thickener.

corella pear small, crisp pear having a distinctive pink blush.

couscous a grain-like cereal product made from semolina.

cream

FRESH also known as pure cream and pouring cream (minimum fat content 35%).

SOUR a thick, commercially cultured soured cream (minimum fat content 35%).

THICKENED a whipping cream (minimum fat content 35%) containing a thickener.

cucumber, lebanese also known as the European or burpless cucumber.

eggs some recipes call for uncooked eggs; exercise caution if salmonella is a problem where you live.

eggplant also known as aubergine.

fish sauce also called naam pla or nuoc naam; made from salted fermented fish, usually anchovies.

five-spice powder fragrant mixture of ground cinnamon, clove, star-anise, sichuan pepper and fennel.

flour, plain an all-purpose flour made from wheat.

garam masala Indian spice mix made up of roast ground clove, cardamom, cinnamon, coriander, fennel and cumin.

ghee clarified butter.

ginger also known as green or root ginger.

gow gee pastry substitute wonton wrappers, spring roll or egg pastry sheets.

green ginger wine beverage 14% alcohol by volume, has the taste of fresh ginger. In cooking, substitute dry (white) vermouth if you prefer, or even an equivalent amount of syrup from a jar of preserved ginger.

kaffir lime leaves aromatic leaves of a small citrus tree.

kumara orange sweet potato.

lemon grass a tall, lemon-tasting, sharp-edged grass.

maple syrup distilled sap of the maple tree.

mesclun an assortment of various edible green leaves.

mince meat also known as ground meat.

mirin a sweet rice wine.

mixed spice a ground-spice blend consisting of allspice, cinnamon and nutmeg.

nashi also called Japanese or Asian pear; resembles a crossbred pear and apple.

non-reactive pan saucepan made of a material that does not react adversely to foods cooked in it.

noodles

BEAN THREAD also known as cellophane noodles.

EGG made from wheat flour and eggs; fresh or dried.

FRESH RICE thick, wide; made from rice and vegetable oil.

HOKKIEN also known as stir-fry noodles.

RICE VERMICELLI also known as rice-flour noodles.

oil

OLIVE made from ripened olives. Extra virgin and virgin are the best quality while extra light or light refers to taste not fat levels.

PEANUT pressed from peanuts.

SESAME made from roasted, crushed, white sesame seeds.

VEGETABLE any oil made from plant rather than animal fats.

onion

GREEN also known as scallion or (incorrectly) shallot.

RED also known as Spanish, red Spanish or Bermuda onion.

oyster sauce made from soy sauce, oysters, brine and salt.

pancetta a salt-cured pork roll; substitute bacon.

passionfruit also known as granadilla; a tropical fruit.

plum sauce made from plums, vinegar, sugar, chillies and spices.

pork, chinese barbecued also called char siew; sold, cooked, in Asian food shops.

prawns also called shrimp.

prosciutto salt-cured, air-dried pressed ham.

pumpkin also called squash.

rice

ARBORIO small round-grain rice good for absorbing a large amount of liquid.

JASMINE aromatic long-grain white rice.

PAPER made from rice paste, stamped into rounds. Dipped in warm water, they become pliable wrappers.

rocket also known as arugula, rugula and rucola.

sambal oelek (also ulek or olek) salty paste made from chillies, garlic and ginger.

sichuan pepper also known as Chinese pepper.

snow peas also called mange tout ("eat all").

soy sauce made from fermented soy beans.

sprouts, bean also known as bean shoots; most common are mung bean, soy bean, alfalfa and snow pea sprouts.

star-anise dried star-shaped pod; seeds taste of aniseed.

stock 1 cup stock (250ml) equals 1 cup water (250ml) plus 1 crumbled stock cube (or 1 teaspoon stock powder), or make fresh stock.

sugar we used coarse, granulated table sugar.

BROWN a soft, fine sugar retaining molasses.

CASTER also called superfine or finely granulated sugar.

PALM fine sugar from the coconut palm; also called gula jawa, gula melaka or jaggery.

RAW natural brown granulated sugar.

tabasco sauce fiery sauce of vinegar, peppers and salt.

tofu also called bean curd.

tahini sesame-seed paste used in Lebanese cooking.

tamarind

CONCENTRATE a ready-to-use tamarind paste.

PULP dehydrated meat of a tamarind pod.

tandoori paste consists of garlic, tamarind, ginger, coriander, chilli and spices.

tat soi also known as rosette pak choy, tai gu choy, Chinese flat cabbage.

vietnamese mint also known as laksa leaves.

vinegar

BALSAMIC made from Italian white wine, then aged.

RED WINE based on fermented red wine.

RICE based on fermented rice.

WHITE WINE made from white wine.

wasabi Japanese horseradish used on sushi or in sauces to add heat and pungency.

watercress member of the mustard family; small round leaves with a peppery flavour.

witlof also known as chicory or Belgian endive.

wonton wrappers substitute gow gee or spring roll sheets.

zucchini also known as courgette.

conversion chart

MEASURES

One Australian metric measuring cup holds approximately 250ml; one Australian metric tablespoon holds 20ml; one Australian metric teaspoon holds 5ml.

The difference between one country's measuring cups and another's is within a two- or three-teaspoon variance, and will not affect your cooking results. North America, New Zealand and the United Kingdom use a 15ml tablespoon.

All cup and spoon measurements are level. The most accurate way of measuring dry ingredients is to weigh them. When measuring liquids, use a clear glass or plastic jug with the metric markings.

We use large eggs with an average weight of 60g.

DRY MEASURES

METRIC	IMPERIAL
15g	½oz
30g	1oz
60g	2oz
90g	3oz
125g	4oz (¼lb)
155g	5oz
185g	6oz
220g	7oz
250g	8oz (½lb)
280g	9oz
315g	10oz
345g	11oz
375g	12oz (¾lb)
410g	13oz
440g	14oz
470g	15oz
500g	16oz (1lb)
750g	24oz (1½lb)
1kg	32oz (2lb)

LIQUID MEASURES

METRIC	IMPERIAL
30ml	1 fluid oz
60ml	2 fluid oz
100ml	3 fluid oz
125ml	4 fluid oz
150ml	5 fluid oz (¼ pint/1 gill)
190ml	6 fluid oz
250ml	8 fluid oz
300ml	10 fluid oz (½ pint)
500ml	16 fluid oz
600ml	20 fluid oz (1 pint)
1000ml (1 litre)	1¾ pints

LENGTH MEASURES

METRIC	IMPERIAL
3mm	⅛in
6mm	¼in
1cm	½in
2cm	¾in
2.5cm	1in
5cm	2in
6cm	2½in
8cm	3in
10cm	4in
13cm	5in
15cm	6in
18cm	7in
20cm	8in
23cm	9in
25cm	10in
28cm	11in
30cm	12in (1ft)

OVEN TEMPERATURES

These oven temperatures are only a guide for conventional ovens. For fan-forced ovens, check the manufacturer's manual.

	°C (CELSIUS)	°F (FAHRENHEIT)	GAS MARK
Very slow	120	250	½
Slow	150	275-300	1-2
Moderately slow	160	325	3
Moderate	180	350-375	4-5
Moderately hot	200	400	6
Hot	220	425-450	7-8
Very hot	240	475	9

index

First published in 2000 by ACP Books, Sydney
Reprinted 2003.

This edition published in 2011 by Bounty Books
a division of Octopus Publishing Group Ltd
Endeavour House, 189 Shaftesbury Avenue,
London WC2H 8JY
www.octopusbooks.co.uk

An Hachette UK Company
www.hachette.co.uk

ISBN: 978-0-753723-20-3

Printed and bound in China